DE PROPRIETATIBUS LITTERARUM

edenda curat

C.H. VAN SCHOONEVELD

Indiana University

Series Practica, 16

THE STYLE OF JOHN WYCLIF'S ENGLISH SERMONS

by

PEGGY ANN KNAPP

1977

MOUTON

THE HAGUE - PARIS

ISBN 90 279 3156 9

Printed in the Netherlands

To the Memory of
Alan Markman

TABLE OF CONTENTS

1

INTRODUCTION

Few men in history can claim the bitter vituperation and the extravagant admiration that has befallen the name of John Wyclif since a stroke on the last day of 1384 took his life. The immediate reaction of the official spokesmen for the Church was to ban his books, discredit his character, and bribe or threaten his followers to abandon his precepts. Until the sixteenth century the histories referred to his 'pernicious' influence. Then the Reformation, zealous to extend its doctrinal claims backward in time, found in Wyclif's life and teaching the very morning star to prefigure its own established day-light. John Foxe's *Book of Martyrs,* with its lurid descriptions of burning Lollards, became the first serious reading for generations of English children.[1] As its influence waned, so did serious interest in Wyclif, until Canon Shirley, writing in 1858, refers to the "dim image of Wyclif . . . without personality or expression".[2] The nineteenth century attempted to atone for its neglect of the Reformer by heaping upon him eulogy after uncritical eulogy. He became in this idiom a human being without faults, a philosopher unmatched in pre-Reformation English history, and a Protestant in every article of his creed. Lately scholars who are interested in discovering sober truths about the Middle Ages have turned their critical methods toward the establishment of an authentic biography for Wyclif's life and a true canon of his works.

Unfortunately much of the evidence is missing or ambiguous. The few documents about him which survive from his lifetime are colored either by his enemies or friends. Those Latin works about which there is no question of Wyclif's authorship are either obscure by reason of their scholastic formalism or so heatedly polemical as to prevent the revelation of any side of him beyond manifest indignation. The list of English works which ought to be called Wyclif's own decreases as scholars uncover historical or paleographical evidence for someone else's authorship. There is, therefore, little which can indicate unerringly what Wyclif was like, and much controversy to add to the aura of mystery which surrounds him. There are probably more biographies of Wyclif than of any other Englishman of the Middle Ages;[3] he is even now an impressive and enigmatic figure.

Although I hesitate to muddy the waters still further, I believe that one useful approach to the enigma of Wyclif's character is the study of his prose style. I do not mean to suggest that all the bothersome problems of motive and intention will vanish with a just appreciation of style. I do think that a modest gain may result from a careful attempt to trace in the more accessible habits of his expression some of his individual modes of conception.

The correction of our knowledge of Wyclif himself, however, is only one reason, perhaps a less important one, for studying his style. The more direct goal of this book is to place Wyclif's prose in a more reasonable position among the prose documents of the late medieval period. Histories of literature have long given Wyclif the unjustified title of 'Father to English prose', primarily on the bases of translations of the Bible which he is no longer believed to have written. The fullest statement of the case is presented by G. P. Krapp in *The Rise of English Literary Prose.*[4] Professor Krapp underemphasizes both the tradition of prose devotional works before Wyclif and the history of medieval preaching, envisioning Wyclif as a lonely pioneer who singlehandedly cleared the way for the achievements of English prose style ever since. R. W. Chambers, in his concern to show the debt of fourteenth century prose to earlier writing, excludes Wyclif's influence because of what he believes to be the failures of the Wycliffite Bible versions.[5] He mentions neither Wyclif's sermons nor his tracts, although they have been found in numerous manuscripts and undoubtedly reached even the illiterate through the spoken words of Wyclif and his party. Since Chambers's book, Wyclif's style was completely neglected until Henry Hargreave's brief essay on the sermons in 1966.

A just assessment of the value of Wyclif's style requires that it be placed in the tradition from which it sprang, while at the same time it be acknowledged for its distinctive achievements. It is a very ambitious task which Wyclif set for himself when he attempted to translate theories which he himself worked out after years of scholarly labor into precepts upon which every unlettered layman might base his faith and mold his life. An unwavering antipathy to the preaching methods of the friars prevented the use of any unBiblical narrative in the sermons, and the choice of the texts for each day of the liturgical year required Wyclif to preach on a wide variety of themes. Perhaps W. W. Shirley's discovery of 'exquisite pathos', 'keen, delicate irony', and 'manly passion' forged into a style which "cannot be read without a feeling of beauty to this hour" is too much to expect; perhaps under such circumstances mere intelligibility may be considered a solid achievement and any further excellences an unlooked-for blessing.

It does seem fitting to outline the main events of Wyclif's career and the main directions of his theological speculation. At least these facts may empower the reader of the sermons to imagine a figure to inhabit the pulpit; at best they modify and are in turn modified by the stylistic features under discussion.

Wyclif was born in Yorkshire, although it is not known definitely where, in the 1320's.[6] It is likely that he lived at Balliol when he went to Oxford, both because that college was founded by near neighbors of the Wyclifs and because in 1358 he briefly held the post of master there. Three years later Wyclif was instituted as rector of Fillingham; he was almost certainly a non-resident, both from there and from his prebend in Westbury, obtained in 1362.

In 1365 a person named 'John de Wyclif' was placed in charge of Canterbury Hall, a recently founded body of mixed monks and seculars. When he was deposed from the office, the unlucky warden was drawn into a legal controversy which dragged on for years and ended in an unsuccessful appeal to the Roman Curia. If the Canterbury warden is the author of these sermons, the unwavering antipathy with which monks are described is given a personal dimension to supplement the doctrinal charges he made against them.

By 1372 Wyclif had earned his doctorate and established his reputation, not only within the university, but among the anti-papal compatriots of John of Gaunt. Two years later he was presented the rectory of Lutterworth by the Crown and appointed a royal envoy to a conference with emissaries of the Pope at Bruges. The meetings ended without a definite settlement, but Wyclif's contact with the papal court left him seriously disillusioned.

The publication of *de Civili Dominio* was probably the reason Wyclif was asked to defend his opinions early in 1377 and certainly the source of the eighteen condemned conclusions for which Pope Gregory XI asked that Wyclif be imprisoned. The University and the English government, however, were equally unwilling to grant the Pope's authority in such matters. The trial was disrupted by an argument between Bishop Courtenay and John of Gaunt, and the papal bulls lay unobserved. In fact, Wyclif continued to wield political influence, supporting Gaunt's claim before Parliament in a breach of sanctuary suit. Wyclif's trial at Lambeth was interrupted by a messenger from Princess Joan of Wales in his behalf and consequently resulted in nothing more than a gentle request that he refrain from discussing certain questions openly.

Meanwhile Wyclif was working out his theological system in a series of Latin treatises which, taken together, are his *Summa de Ente*; at the same time he was beginning to have influence outside Oxford through priests who took his theology and ecclesiastical criticism directly to their local parishes. Both projects solidified his hostile critics, for the University was under increasingly great pressure to give its condemnation of doctrine which struck at the heart of the medieval ecclesiastical system, and John of Gaunt was unable to maintain his patronage of an officially heretical theologian. The situation was further worsened when John Ball, a leader in the Peasants' Revolt, claimed Wyclif for his instructor. A council at Blackfriars in 1382 proscribed twenty-four articles from Wyclif's works and, with some difficulty, forced the University to publish the condemnation and prohibit open teaching by Wyclif's men. Wyclif himself retired to Lutterworth where, until his death in December, 1384, he wrote in both Latin and English, superintended the work of his 'Poor Priests' (probably a collection of individuals rather than an organized sect), directed a translation of the Bible, and performed pastoral duties for his parishoners. A stroke in 1384 caused his death, and shortly thereafter the Council of Constance ordered his bones dug up and burned and his theological treatises suppressed.

Archbishop Courtenay untiringly bribed, threatened, and as a last resort executed Wyclif's disciples with a good deal of success. Yet it was necessary at times throughout the fifteenth century to direct sermons, plays, and legal actions against the Lollards.[7] Wyclif's books were burned in Prague in 1410 and it was unquestionably Wyclif's theology which sent John Hus to the stake and precipitated a religious civil war in Bohemia. Some commentators see a direct line from Wyclif to the English Reformation; others claim he did 'everything possible' to delay it.[8] In any case, his work became the center of a controversy which touched most phases of medieval life.

In order to describe the doctrine which caused such havoc within the Church, the University, and the English state it is necessary to outline the controversy which rendered Oxford "a scene of immense intellectual activity . . . which had more contact with the religious and political life of the country at large than was the case with the Parisian scholasticism of the preceding century".[9] The harmony between philosophy and theology toward which medieval thinkers necessarily strained, and even such as Abelard believed it possible to achieve,[10] was in large measure attained by Albertus Magnus and Thomas Aquinas in the thirteenth century. The resulting intellectual repose was, however, short-lived; Duns Scotus and William of Occam soon revived nominalism so forcefully that the fourteenth century could not take Aquinas's solution for granted. Although Occam's views were solemnly condemned by the University of Paris in 1340, they gained influence so quickly that by Wyclif's lifetime they were clearly ascendent. The nominalism, or conceptualism,[11] of Occam resulted, whatever its creator's intentions, in a burst of critical and skeptical writing by his followers. To Wyclif nominalism looked like heresy. Like his countryman Thomas Bradwardine, he saw in the issue of Occam's logic a form of the Pelagian heresy which placed too great an emphasis on individual human will. Instead of turning to the moderate view of Aquinas, however, Wyclif sought in the Platonic realism of Augustine the foundations of his inflexibly realistic position. Far from asserting unlimited freedom of speculation within the Church, Wyclif was seeking an older and more orthodox authority from which to argue his case. He posited that all things have their being as part of God's being, and therefore share his eternality and indestructibility, "so that anything, once in being, could not but be".[12] The realistic doctrine that no created thing may be annihilated gradually forced him to examine and discard the position of the Church on the Eucharist, which postulated the substitution of Christ's body for the bread of the mass and consequently, the destruction of the substance of the bread. Thus he was caught in the irony which must account for many heterodoxies, namely, "that he utilized a metaphysical principle, which he thought of as a guard against heretical opinions, but by which he was himself being inexorably driven into open heresy".[13]

For this break with orthodoxy Wyclif might be remembered as a minor scholastic figure whose views looked backwards to a pre-Abelardian settlement. The enormous controversy connected with his name arose because he saw and published the practical consequences of his theological system. The theory of dominion follows from the consideration of creation according to realism: God's will, far from arbitrary as Occam had claimed, is determined by his nature, and man's lordship is derived directly from God's in the feudal manner. Such, by the way, does not suggest the communistic or egalitarian ideas commonly imputed to Wyclif by nineteenth-century critics, nor did Wyclif ever hint that it should. Dominion as Wyclif explained it in no way jeopardized the proprietary claims of the nobility; the dominion of the man in grace was not to be worked out in human society.[14] It was against the claims of the Pope to temporal power and ownership that Wyclif's doctrine militated. The first condemned conclusions (1377) all dealt with this issue. As Wyclif faced the consequences of his viewpoint, he gradually came to count the testimony of the Church, especially since the donation of Constantine which marked the end of her Apostolic purity, for less and less, and the authority of the Bible for more and more.[15] Once the sole sufficiency of scripture became his established point of departure, the whole conduct of Christendom lay open to re-examination. The sermons which are my texts perform in English what Latin treatises many times their bulk demonstrate to the learned community, i.e. that the Church has strayed from the simple piety of Christ, sought earthly possessions, and forfeited her claim to holiness. If the simple people would know God, they must go directly to His Word. Thus from his own extreme interpretation of philosophical realism, Wyclif moves to a belief in the dominion of all created beings, and from that to the sufficiency of the Bible to supply the needs of Christian faith. Wyclif is often called unsystematic because so much of what he wrote was produced to meet specific occasions, but, whether or not he ordered it in his own publications, his view is signally amenable to systematization. He is, in fact, a man with what our generation calls a radical idea.

The five groups of English sermons (MS Bodleian 788) edited by Thomas Arnold have long been accepted as the most reliable guide to the establishment of the English Wyclif canon. They were so used by E. P.

Jones,[16] whose opinion was not exhaustively disputed until an article by E. W. Talbert questioned the dating and authorship of the sermons on the grounds of their references to contemporary events.[17] His evidence consists of five types of allusion "(1) references to the Papacy, since the Lollards censured Gregory XI, praised Urban VI, but attacked him in turn as the Schism developed; (2), references to the crusade of Bishop Spenser, proclaimed in March, 1381 and completed in September, 1383; (3) statements which may be interpreted as referring to events in the seventies; (4) statements which indicate that Oxford was an unmolested seat of Lollardy; (5) references to events after Wyclif's death'.[18] The first three categories allow very specific dating, and Talbert's conclusions placing the original composition of the sermons earlier than the commonly accepted dates seem fully justified. Nor are these early dates inconsistent with the theory that the English sermons were prepared for preaching at Luttterworth, for that rectory was in Wyclif's care from 1374 until his death. The references to unmolested Lollardy at Oxford are much more questionable. The two passages are worded thus: "Siche doutes we shulden sende to þe scole of Oxenforde, and we shulden wite wel bi God þat dyverse feiþis in a man, now on and now oþer, make no feiþ in him, 3he, 3if þe tyme be dyverse þat þis feiþ þus comeþ or goiþ. And þus may God encrese oure feiþ, and we by synne enfeblen oure feiþ . . ." (I, 93-94)[19] and "And leve we to 3onge men scole tretynge of þis matere, but 3it men douten what moveþ God to wiþdrawe his grace fro men, and to lette þis seed for to growe, as he shewiþ it in parablis" (I, 105). In both cases the force of the argument is not so much that matters will be decided correctly (i.e. in favor of Lollard contentions) at Oxford, but that the discussions are technical and more suitable for debate among scholars than they are necessary for faith. If this is their meaning, these passages fall into place among a very large group of remarks which discourage subtle speculation and emphasize the adequacy of the Bible to explain all matters necessary to true faith. The relevance they have to the ascription of the sermons to the time when Lollardy was unchecked at Oxford is tenuous.

There are three passages considered by Talbert to refer to dates after Wyclif's death in 1384. The first is a reference to the suppression of an English Bible by statute and the acquiescence of 'kyn3tis' who were bribed to confirm it. "Þei [oure heye preestis and oure newe religiouse] dredden hem þat Goddis law shal quyken after þis, and herfore þei maken statutis, stable as a stoon; and þei geten graunt of kny3tis to confermen hem . . . . Wel Y wote þat kny3tis tooken gold in þis case . . ." (I, 129). The Constitutions of Oxford, formulated in 1407 and confirmed by Parliament in 1411, prohibited the translation and preaching of the Bible without express ecclesiastical sanction. It seems likely that these constitutions are referred to by the sermon. The second allusion is less specific. It alleges that true men are disuaded from preaching God's word "by 3yvyng of þer money, and of greet benefices" (II, 132-133). Talbert takes this as a reference to the recantations of some prominent Lollards in the 1390's and early fifteenth century. Nevertheless, Archbishop Sudbury had enjoined silence from Wyclif as early as 1377, and may have used the lure of lucrative benefices to check the rise of Lollardy before the famous recantations of the nineties. The third passage is dated by a remark said to have been made in Parliament in 1395 by John of Gaunt, but the evidence for such a specific dating of John's opinion is less impressive than the certain knowledge that he and many other knights supported Wyclif's views over a period of many years. The wording of the sermon, "But too confort is of kny$_3$tis, þat þei savoren myche þe gospel and han wille to rede in Englishe þe gospel of Cristis liif" (I, 209), does not argue for a specific defense as much as a continuing support of Lollard doctrine on the Bible.

The wide range of dates for the composition of these sermons suggested by Talbert's study allows several explanations. It may be that the whole corpus was written by a man whose life spanned the events mentioned in the sermons, and whose views were very deeply influenced by the whole range of Wyclif's expressed opinions. Although such a theory is impossible to disprove, its acceptance involves the repudiation of Thomas Netter's contemporary opinion and nearly six centuries of tradition.[20]

Professor Talbert's own conclusion is that the Bodleian 788 manuscript which Arnold makes the basis of his edition "probably represents one culmination of a process of compilation, revision, and addition which a collection of sermons underwent at the hands of Lollards during the years from ca. 1377 to ca. 1412". This may, of course, be the case, but the evidence for such a complicated theory seems to me rather thin. The only unequivocal allusion to an event after Wyclif's death is that which refers to the Constitutions of Oxford (1407) and their confirmation by Parliament (1411), and even this 'graunt of kny$_3$tis' might refer to a preliminary agreement between the Church and John of Gaunt's party, for Gaunt is known to have warned Wyclif to be silent more than three years before the Reformer's death. Moreover, such a theory does not explain the admitted uniformity of the style of the sermons.

It is also possible that Wyclif composed and later revised the sermons himself, but that the fairly late Bodleian 788 manuscript may contain an occasional interpolation from after 1384. Completeness was one of Arnold's reasons for choosing Bodl. 788 as his base manuscript,[21] but this virtue may have been attained at the loss of absolute authenticity. A study of the other manuscripts as Talbert suggested would be necessary to reveal the evidence for such a proposition. It is known that Wyclif edited his own Latin sermons during his residence at Lutterworth and that he considered them important for the edification of the Church.[22] The collection and revision of his English sermons, therefore, would be consistent with his practice and his stated aims.

The feeling engendered by his serious illness that his life was nearing an end may have prompted him to prepare his sermons for helps to the younger men whose preaching he had been encouraging. The fact that interpolated passages, if there be such, do not differ stylistically from the original material creates no great difficulty. A man who had been reading Wyclif's words and accepting his doctrine might well produce a short passage which would not deviate noticeably from the rest of the text. This approach to the sermons accounts for their traditional ascription to Wyclif, their single conformity to his doctrinal system, their widely varied allusions to events, and their uniformity of style. I offer this explanation of the composition of the sermons because it seems to account for more of the established facts than any other. If new evidence reveals that Wyclif did not produce the English sermons in this form, very little of what I have observed about their style will have to be reconsidered, only those few occasions when I have linked stylistic features with events in Wyclif's biography. The theology and moral instruction of these sermons is Wyclif's, whether in his words or someone else's, and the marks of the style, whether his or another's, retain their excellence and exert their influence on subsequent generations of English writers.

[1] John Foxe, *The Book of Martyrs,* 3 vols. (London, 1641).

[2] W. W. Shirley, in his Introduction to *Fasciculi Zizaniorum* (*Rolls Series*) (London, 1858), p. xivi.

[3] K. B. McFarlane, *John Wyclif and the Beginnings of English Non-conformity* (London, 1952), p. 10.

[4] (Oxford, New York, 1915).

[5] *On the Continuity of English Prose* (*EETS,* O S 186) (London, 1932).

[6] The chronology of Wyclif's life I have taken from H. B. Workman, *John Wyclif: A Study of the English Medieval Church* (Oxford, 1926). It is the later of the two definitive biographies, the other being G. V. Lechler's *John Wycliffe and His English Precursors,* trans. J. Lorimer (London, 1884).

[7] See Cecillia Cutts, "The Croxton Play: An Anti-Lollard Piece", *MLQ* (March 1944), 45-60.

[8] McFarlane, in his *John Wyclif . . .*, disclaims Wyclif's influence on the Reformation; see pp. 186-188. Lechler, Workman, and Trevelyan, *England in the Age of Wycliffe* (London, 1904), tend to overstate it. A moderate view is found in James Gairdner's four-volume study *Lollardy and the Reformation in England* (London, 1908-1913).

[9] Hastings Rashdall, *Medieval Universities* (Powicke and Emden: Oxford, 1936), pp. 267-268.

[10] R. L. Poole, *Illustrations of the History of Medieval Thought and Learning,* 2nd ed. (London, 1920), p. 116. The history of scholasticism is discussed in Poole's book and in Julius Weinberg's *A Short History of Medieval Philosophy* (Princeton, 1964).

[11] See Weinberg, *A Short History,* pp. 235-265.

[12] Gordon Leff, *Heresy in the Later Middle Ages* (Manchester, 1967), II, 510.

[13] J. A. Robson, *Wyclif and the Oxford Schools* (Cambridge, England, 1961), p. 187.
[14] Poole, *Illustrations,* p. 261.
[15] Matthew Spinka, *Advocates of Reform,* XIV (1953), p. 69.
[16] "Authenticity of Some English Works Ascribed to Wyclif", *Anglia* XXX (1907), pp. 261-268.
[17] "The Date of the Composition of the English Wycliffite Collection of Sermons", *Speculum,* XII (October 1937), 464-474.
[18] Talbert, "The Date of the Composition", p. 468.
[19] All references to the English sermons are from Thomas Arnold's edition of the *Select English Works* (Oxford, 1869-1871). There are three volumes in the series, the first two of which contain the sermons.
[20] *Fasciculi Zizaniorum,* p. 59.
[21] *Select English Works,* I, xxi.
[22] "Sermones", *Latin Works,* IV, ed. J. Loserth (Wyclif Society: London, 1887), Part I, v.

2

THE CONTEXT: FOURTEENTH-CENTURY PROSE

It is possible to imagine a lyric poem so well developed in form and so universal in subject as to be equally appropriate to any time or place. For such a masterpiece the establishment of a context, although helpful, would be secondary in understanding the poem. Prose is almost never like that. Instead it is, as J. S. Phillimore put it, "an institution, part of the equipment of a civilization, part of its heritable wealth".[1] Of central importance, then, to the study of Wyclif's sermon style, is an account of the 'heritable wealth' which the Reformer received from his predecessors and contemporaries.

The two main streams which begin to flow together in the late fourteenth century to constitute English prose are the styles of great mystics and those of workmanlike translators. The mystics, who will be represented here by Richard Rolle, the author of the *Cloud of Unknowing,* Dame Julian of Norwich, and Walter Hilton, had a prose tradition available to them, possibly a very old one extending back to the writings of Alfred.[2] The translators had their native speech to guide them, but it was their task to fashion it to literary conciseness and clarity. John Trevisa and the translator of *Mandeville's Travels* will represent two solutions for this. All the while another group, the preachers, were meeting the requirements of their offices in prose. The second half of the fourteenth century saw an enormous surge of interest in sermon-making by those whose duty was overseeing the work of local priests and by the priests themselves. The instruction books written in English are as different from each other as *Speculum Christiani* and Mirk's *Festial,* and the sermons are even more widely varied. Together these three influences—the mystics, the translators, and the preachers—form a context for Wyclif's work, against which his debts may be acknowledged and his true innovations calculated.

The mystics would appear as a group, I think, even if their special characteristics as believers did not set them apart: they write very similar English. It is possible that they read and influenced each other, but it is also possible that the similarity of their experiences demanded somewhat similar expressions. Certainly the highly emotional tone, the abundance of personal reference, and the variety of effects achieved are appropriate to an attempt to convey direct religious experience.

Rolle's style is actually many different styles, as many as the hermit had need of to express his various intentions in writing.[3] Some share the impulse of lyric poetry to present the ineffable, but others are designed primarily to instruct. Even the most straight-forward discourse, however, reveals a craftsman's care for the effects of language. This care asserts itself in three major ways: metaphor, alliteration, and parallelism.

At a very elementary level, the tendency to use metaphor appears, much as it would in bestiary collections, in a likening of the man burdened with sin to the stork, whose heavy body prevents his flight: "thay may noght flye to lufe and contemplacyone of God þay are so chargede wyth othyre affeccyons and othire vanytes" (p. 9). Metaphor can also be so rich with meaning that only it, and even it imperfectly, is able to suggest the nature of the writer's experience. The image of fire returns time and again at crucial points in Rolle's treatises, when all else has been said directly; for example, "þat saule þat es purede in þe fyre of lufe of Godd, þat all erthely sauour as brynte owte of it . . ." (p. 16).

Although it is scarcely noticeable in cursory readings, there is a subtle rhythm pervading much of Rolle's work. This is partly the effect of the management of parallel constructions and partly of a sparing use of alliteration within phrases, such as "pertynere of þe payne" and "þe flesche be felawe of þe joy" (p. 15). In combination, parallelism and alliteration produce effects like this: "fillis it and fedis it with swetnes of hymselfe" (p. 18).

There are parallel constructions in Rolle's works which simply organize the narrative. "Whare-fare, accordandly Arystotill sais þat some fowheles are . . .", forms the beginning of a paragraph in which the next three sentences all begin with 'some are'. A similar device is used in the treatise on the commandments: "The nam of Gode es takyn in vayne one many maners. With herte, with mouthe, with werke. With herte . . . with-owttene grace in sawle. With mouthe . . . when we honour God with oure lippys . . . . With werke . . . for they feyne gud dede with-owttene, and þey erre with-owtten charyte . . ." (p. 10). Here the parallelism is strengthened, not only by the repetition of 'herte', 'mouthe', and 'werke' at the beginning of the explanatory sentences but also by the heavy repetition of 'with' and 'with-owttene' in various places in each sentence. A somewhat different use of 'with-owttene' appears in another form of parallelism in "The Onehede of God": "Oure Lorde Godd es ane endles beynge with-owtten chaungynge, all-mighty with-owttene faylynge, souerayne wysdome, lyghte, sofastenes with-owtten errour or myrknes" (p. 14), where the preposition keeps its place and the number of elements it relates is varied.

Although Rolle seldom used the completely synonymous word pairs or triplets so common among translators from Latin in the fourteenth century, he does very often link several similar words or phrases, either conjunctively ("þis is þe fredom and þe lordchipe, dygnyte and þe wyrchipp þat a manes saule hase . . ." [p. 15]) or disjunctively ("fulfillede perfytely, contenually, ne hally in þis lyfe" [p. 14]). Used for the summation of a whole paragraph, the device produces a fine sense of climax. "The fyrste manere es nedfull vs to do, the tothire we awe to do, the thirde es perfeccyone" (p. 10).

The author of the *Cloud of Unknowing*[4] shows similar care for effects of language. Like Rolle's, his crucial points must often be made figuratively, and like Rolle's, his tone is personal rather than academic. The author seems to have a specific correspondent in mind, and often anticipates his doubts and misunderstandings, giving him questions in dialogue form. There is liberal use of 'I', rhetorical question, and exclamation. These are common devices in an oral style, and the author seems to have expected his book to be heard as well as read.[5]

The writer's metaphors are both striking and carefully developed. To the rather common figure of God as 'goostly spouse' he adds: "But oo þing I telle þee: he is a gelous louer & suffreþ no felawschip, & him list not worche in þi wille bot ȝif he be only wiþ þee bi hym-self" (p. 15). His learning emerges in his likening the length of his book to an 'athomus', which according to astronomers, "is þe leest partie of tyme". Once explained, the 'athomus' appears again, "For euen so many willinges or desiringes . . . may be & aren in one oure in þi wille, as aren athomus in one oure" (p. 18). The loveliest and fullest of his figures–that from which the book takes its title–appears again and again, constantly gathering associations. "& wene not, for I clepe it a derknes or a cloude, þat it be any cloude congelid of þe humours þat fleen in þe ayre, ne ȝit any derknes soche as is in þin house on niȝtes, when þi candel is oute. For soche a derknes & soche a cloude maist þou ymagin wiþ coriouste of witte, for to bere before þin iȝen in þe liȝtest day of somer, & also aȝenswarde in þe derkist niȝt of wynter þou mayst ymagin a clere schinyng liȝt" (p. 23); "& smyte apon þat þicke cloude of vnknowyng wiþ a scharp darte of longing loue" (p. 26).

There are also frequent alliterative effects in the work, although they do not disturb the prose rhythm. Usually the alliterating words are a noun and its modifier ('tiþing tellers' [p. 2], 'a besi beholding' [p. 13]), a verb and adverb ('stonde stifly' [p. 13]), or balanced expressions ('þi scheeld & þi spere' [p. 28]).

The author of the *Cloud* is a master of the effects of balance and antithesis. Although there are cases of word pairs which are simply synonymous ("he mad þee & wrouȝt þee' [p. 13]), there are usually two ideas present ("þe cours & þe maner" [p. 13], "how lystly and how graciously" [p. 14]). Sometimes a variation is effected by using three balanced terms: "stonde stifly in þe state & þe degree & in þe forurme of leuying . . ." (p. 13). At other times whole phrases are balanced, as in the figure already quoted when both 'derknes' and 'cloude' are paired, as are 'liȝtest day of somer' and 'derkist ni$_{3}$t of wynter' (p. 23). In another place a pair of clauses are balanced: "Bot what schalt þou do, & how schalt þou put?" (p. 16).

Antithesis of one term, phrase, or clause against another is also common: "Lette not þerfore, bot trauayle þer-in tyl þou fele lyst" (p. 16). A further refinement appears in the addition of a phrase to the second member: "not only in actyue leuyng, bot in þe souereinnest pointe of contemplatife leuyng" (p. 2). Later, balance was used to structure the whole sentence: "a man falleþ depper & depper in synne, & ferþer & ferþer fro God . . . a man euer-more riseþ hier & hier fro synne, & nerer & nerer vnto God" (p. 20).

This author also has a talent for epigram. In the small sample of prose I have considered there are two strikingly condensed statements: "In oo litel tyme, as litel as it is, may heuen be wonne & lost" (p. 20), and "For tyme is maad for man, & not man for tyme" (p. 20).

Most of the literary devices developed in the writings of Rolle and the author of the *Cloud* are present also in the style of Dame Julian, anchoress of Norwich.[6] The *Revelations of Divine Love* is an intensely personal account of that writer's own 'shewings' from God, and, as would be expected, she uses 'I' and 'me' heavily, quotes scarcely anything, reports dialogue between her soul and God, and makes little attempt to arrive at abstract statements. The special strength of her style is its ability to imbue the mystic experience with a homely tenderness without rendering it less than fully spiritual.

Metaphoric expressions, which she calls "shewings or bodily examples", are woven in her distinctive fashion. Christ "is our clothing that for love wrappeth us, claspeth us, and encloseth us for tender love . . ." (p. 12). In another variation, this figure becomes, "For as the body is clad in the cloth, and the flesh in the skin, and the bones in the flesh, and the heart in the whole, so are we, soul and body, clad in the Goodness of God, and enclosed" (p. 14). The love of Christ is also embodied in the metaphoric 'solemn King' or 'great Lord' who gives a servant the finest gift, that of his true friendship, "with a glad cheer, both privately and in company" (p. 16).

Although there are many examples of paired epithets or phrases in *Revelations,* there are more commonly groups of three synonymous terms. For example, "a helpless soul come to Him simply and plainly and homely" (p. 11), "how much and how sweetly, and how tenderly our Maker loveth us" (p. 14), and "this high, overpassing, inestimable love . . ." (p. 14). A triple balance of clauses often creates a sense of progression in the narrative, as in "It quickeneth our soul . . . . It is nearest in nature . . . for it is the same grace" (p. 13), and "the first is that God made it, the second is that God loveth it, the third, that God keepeth it. But what is to me verily the Maker, the Keeper, and the Lover,–I cannot tell . . ." (p. 10). Sometimes the parallelism extends to unifying paragraphs, as in chapter six, where seven consecutive sentences begin with 'For'.

Dame Julian also exhibits an undulating rhythm more common in poetry than prose. It is created with variation of the function of a word or phrase, as "For the Trinity is God: God is the Trinity; the Trinity is our Maker and Keeper, the Trinity is our everlasting love and everlasting joy and bliss . . ." (p. 8), and "For our natural Will is to have God, and the Good Will of God is to have us . . ." (p. 14). In descriptive matter this rhythm is created with variation in the visual suggestion as well. This rather long passage combines many of the stylistic features already discussed and gives an idea of how vividly Dame Julian was able to perceive her visions and how aptly she compares them with ordinary sights.

> The great drops of blood fell down from under the Garland like pellots, seeming as it had come out of the veins; and in the coming out they were brown-red, for the blood was full thick; and in the spreading-abroad they were bright red; and when they came to the brows, then they vanished; notwithstanding, the bleeding continued till many things were seen and understood. The fairness and the lifelikeness is nothing but the same; the plenteousness is like to the drops of water that fall off the eaves after a great shower of rain, that fell so thick that no man may number them with bodily wit; and for the roundness, they were like to the scale of herring, in the spreading on the forehead. These three came to my mind in the time: pellots, for roundness, in the coming out of the blood; the scale of herring in the spreading in the forehead, for roundness, the drops off eaves, for the plenteousness innumerable (p. 16).

Walter Hilton's prose in *Scala Perfection* marks a sharp departure from that of the other mystics.[7] The subjects and thoughts are remarkably similar, but their expression by Hilton is more literal and less poetic. Heavy alliteration, parallels and balances in phrasing, antithesis, and rhythmic repetition are rare. The sense of dramatic personal experience is not absent in Hilton, but is no longer the organizing principle of the treatise, as in Rolle or Dame Julian. Instead Hilton divides his text logically, treating the various aspects of contemplative life in turn, and making his answers to objections much in the manner of the 'university preachers'.[8]

Hilton's approach requires him to quote authority frequently. This he does in Latin, with an original translation following. The Bible is his most frequent source, but occasionally the Fathers do appear. These passages are in an altogether different spirit from Rolle's snatches of Scripture, which seem to have been chosen for the mood they convey, or Dame Julian's three lyric cries, the only quotations in her *Revelations.* Hilton offers Scripture as evidence; he is writing in order to instruct and convince as well as to share his own ecstasy and inspire a follower.

This does not mean, however, that his style lacks warmth or imagination. There is still the direct address to a listener as 'thou', the frequent citation of the writer's own experience or insight, and an adaptation of everyday language generously sprinkled with metaphors. Often his images are simply brief expressions which quickly evoke a more vivid and homely tone than a learned term would. For example: a Christian should be "truly to3ned" to God (ch. 1), discursive learning is "but a figure & a shadowe" of true contemplation (ch. IV), contemplation is "the propre well of our lorde/ to the which cometh none alien" (ch. IV), and knowledge alone "is but mater unsavery & cold" (ch. IV). If something disturbs the contemplative state, the Christian should pray that Christ will "with his blessyng turne the water in to wyne as he dide at the prayer of his moder" (ch. IV).

The other kind of metaphor Hilton employs frequently is carefully developed to show all the points of similarity between tenor and vehicle. In such a way he explains a basic mystic figure of burning, insisting that God's fire is one of purification from sin, of dissolving the heart into sweetness, and of leaving the soul malleable under the demands of God's will (ch. V). An analogy of clothing becomes "but that thou shold know that the cause of thy bodely clothyng is that thou myghte the beter come to ghostly clothing/ and as thy body is clotyd fro bodely convention of men/ right soo that thyn hert myght be enclosed from flethly loves & dredes of al erthly thynges" (ch. I).

While the prose of the English mystics was developing a highly personal and poetic style, which nevertheless, as Hilton's case shows, was capable of modification toward straightforward exposition, another group of writers was creating English expository prose through translation. A translator, obviously, is less free to create the large aspects of style, such as organization and figurative treatment, than the original author, but in the Middle Ages he considered his latitude in expanding and explaining his source very wide. We may, therefore, justly speak of Trevisa and the translator of *Mandeville's Travels* as English prose stylists.

The translator of the *Travels*[9] seems not to be over-concerned with niceties of prose style. He is repetitious without the effect of strengthening a remark, and he is a little unsure of the normal structure of the language. (Consider his use, in the same sentence, of 'more cool' and 'more hotter', and the uncertain syntax here: "that every Man may see well, and not irk one another" [p. 8]). He never uses a single word where a pair or triplet can be substituted. Unlike the balanced pairs of the *Cloud*, a second word seldom expresses a second idea, as in Mandeville's "make it to ben cryed & pronounced" (p. 2), "the thing that is proclaimed & pronounced" (p. 2), "I haue seen & beholden" (p. 8), and "the customs & manneres & dyuersitees of contrees" (p. 10).

Yet few things are more obvious to the casual reader than that it is fun to read the book. The ingenuousness and candor of the manner is augmented by the author or translator's faults as a stylist. The very wordiness of this explanation, for example, conjures up an excited teller for the reader's imagination: "And the ouerthwart pece was of palme, for in the olde testament, it was ordeyned þat whan on was ouercommen he scholde be crowned with palme. And for þei trowed þat thei hadden the victorye of christ Jhesus, þerfore made þei the ouerthwart pece of palme" (p. 6-7). And again in this: "And the glass þat is made of þat grauell, ȝif it be don aȝen in to the grauell it turneth anon in to grauell as it was first" (p. 20). Perhaps he is a little too helpful when he explains the meaning of 'Jonkes' to be 'Rushes' twice in two pages.

His words seem to follow his very train of thought, without the stifling influence of connections and subordinations. The sentence structures he employs are mainly coordinate, and the reader must often conjecture exactly what relationship is implied between clauses. A paragraph on the practices of the Greek Church is interrupted by indignation toward Western Catholicism: "And þei [the Greeks] sey also þat vsury is no dedly synne. And þei sellen benefices of holy chirche & so don men in oþere places, god amende it whan his wille is, And þat is gret sclaundre. For now is Simonye kyng crouned in holy chirche, god amende it for his mercy" (p. 12). The city of Satalia in Cypress boasts a legend about a hideous head, begotten on a corpse, which caused the loss of the city to be reported thus: "[it] als swythe fleigh aboute the cytee & the contree & sone after the cytee sank down & þere ben manye perilouse passages . . ." (p. 17). One is left to wonder if the passages are rocky perils to ships or dangers from evil spirits.

The translations of John Trevisa are also wordy, but no one would call them ingenuous.[10] Like Mandeville's translator, Trevisa is anxious to find an exact English synonym for his source, and also like him, he often supplies two or three words just to be sure. Such expressions as "to expowne and declare" (p. 12), "matrimonye and wedlok" (p. 14), and "dystroy, waste, and consume" (p. 25), are merely different renderings of the same idea. But now and then his word pairs create a rhythm: ". . . after due and iuste barkynge, ye shall fele bytynge" (p. 19), and "that ye begyle not and deceyue the quycke . . ." (p. 23). Trevisa can also make skillfull use of antithesis: "nor we wrote them not, but God sente them, and the holy gooste spake them", and ". . . he dydde hit not for any couetousnesse, but of Goddelye zeale, not of ambition, but of deuoute relygyon" (p. 22).

Figurative expressions are few, brief, and rather ordinary in content, but they have the virtue of seeming to arise naturally in the dialogue. For example, the knight replies to a new point introduced by the clerk: "Ye awake the slepynge dogge, and dryue me to speake otherwyse than I thoughte before to do. *Cleri:* Lette the hounde wake and barke" (p. 19). Later the clerk protests that the state does not protect him: ". . . ye tere & hale away my flesshe and my skynne, and that ye calle saufgarde" (p. 24), and is answered "the kynges strength is to you in stede of a stronge walle" (p. 25).

The sentence patterns Trevisa employs are such that a careful student can identify his prose quite confidently.[11] In most cases they coincide with modern usage in the placement of subject, verb, and object. (Two exceptions are "yet gotte I not so profounde lernynge", [p. 1], and "priuileges be to you granted by kynges" [p. 34]). The placement of adjectives and adverbs is the distinctive thing; e.g., "more homely and playner fascion" (p. 1), and "sikerly to slepe" (p. 26).

Both the devotional prose of the mystics and the plainer attempts of the translators undoubtedly influenced the efforts of medieval preachers; but one need not assume that they did so directly, for the period under discussion is full of helps for the parish priest. The fourteenth century is the age of manuals for preachers to help them compose for the pulpit and instruct through the confessional. The style, or styles, of these instruction books, and of individual sermons, preached, or at least composed, during this period should complete the account of features common in late fourteenth-century prose.

The collection of Middle English sermons found in a manuscript edited under the title *Middle English Sermons* for the Early English Text Society[12] allows the conclusion that sermon writers chose between three major preaching styles. The 'old' method consisted in rather formless Biblical exegesis, the 'modern' or 'university' in formal divisions and proofs, and the 'friars' in the heavy use of exempla.[13] There are compromises, but one type of organization is generally dominant. The three varieties have more than their method of organization to differentiate them. The sophistication of the thought and style of the body of these sermons makes it clear that in general the 'modern' style was used for learned and the 'old' and *exempla* styles for popular audiences.

The 'old' style is the less frequently preserved, probably because it was preached by someone less likely to be able to have his work reproduced, but it may have been heard oftener by the average English parishoner. The old style sermons included in the collection (numbers 23-30) are short and unpretentious. The tone is homely, set by the simple beginning words: "The gospell of þis day telliþ us . . ." (p.133). The text for the day, and additional quotations from the Bible, are entirely in English, and occur within the preacher's own sentences. The sentence structures are varied and competent to clarify relationships between clauses, but not rhythmic or especially dramatic. There are no flashes of figurative speech or brilliant antithesis.

The 'modern' style, on the other hand, is an exercise in aesthetics. At worst it is written by formula, with only a specious coherence and no real insight. At best it is a fine performance, weaving together the divisions and their proofs so that formalism is forgotten. In common with the older type is an affirmation by the preacher that he is speaking rather than writing. All the sermons contain 'I' and 'thou', rhetorical questions, exclamations, and other evidences of oral style, and some put words into the listeners' mouths for the preacher to answer.

The common practice among 'modern' preachers is to quote abundantly from the Fathers as well as the Bible. Sometimes these quotations appear only in Latin, sometimes in Latin and in English. We need not suppose, however, that they were not translated unless the English version appears, for it may have been taken for granted that the preacher would translate as he preached.

Assuming that it is unfinished in this manuscript rather than structurally flawed, Sermon 39 provides a revealing glimpse of the dignity and learning it was possible for a noble audience to hear from the fourteenth-century pulpit. The preacher begins by announcing his text and offering a prayer for the success of his message. To provide an introduction, he discusses an Old Testament passage, showing its relevance to his subject. Another prayer for the preacher and people is made. The text is then divided into four 'questions' and the first of these into subdivisions, each supported with quotations from scripture, the Fathers, and even Horace and Boethius. The intellectual orientation of his method is clear from his own words: "So it may fully þan be concluded as a trouthe . . ." (p. 222). It is in the interest of presenting evidence and conclusions that each point is offered.

The mechanical process of supplying quotations for each subdivision is adroitly handled in this sermon. Sometimes the quoted words appear before, sometimes after, the reference. They are often, but not always, given in both Latin and English. Long passages, like that from Exodus in the introduction, are combined with the preacher's comments so that the story seems told rather than quoted. In no case, however, is any question about a source allowed to remain unanswered.

The preacher provides a good deal of purely factual knowledge connected with his text. He supplies information about the customs of the Far East, and assumes that his listeners will raise objections for him to settle (p. 226). He discusses the peculiarities of Christ's natal star with an obvious knowledge of astronomy. He even supplies (from Isidore's *Ethymologiarum*) the fact that dromedaries can travel one hundred miles a day. His tone in these matters is scholarly, but not condescending.

The diction and syntax this preacher employs, reinforce the impression of sophistication and dignity he creates by his formal method. Christ is addressed in the opening prayer as "most wisse and discrete, rewlyng prudently al þing!" (p. 220), and Moses is referred to as a 'curious philosopher' (p. 221). Terms like 'contemplacioun' and 'incarnacion' are used without definition (p. 222). The preacher's sentences are varied in length and complexity, and exhibit the frequent use of verbal phrases where less polished Middle English writers would probably use clauses, as ". . . þan oure Lord spake to Moyses, repressyng his presumpcion, seyng on þis wize . . ." (p. 221). He uses balanced structures within a sentence: ". . . noþer personell auctorite, science, oþur naturall sotelte, noþur perfite lyvynge in contemplacion shuld cause . . ." (p. 222); and among sentences, "It is ful wondurfull þat God . . . . Also it is full wondurfull how . . . . It is also a full gret wondur . . . . And also it is a gret marveyll . . ." (pp. 222-223). A skilfully handled figure is carried over from the Old Testament text: we must avoid being too "inquisitiff in oure own wittis, for God forbedeþ it and seyþ to euerych of vs þise wordes, 'Com þou no nere hidurward . . . but raþur' seyþ God, 'doþ of þi shoes of þi feete' " (p. 223).

The one Table of *Speculum Christiani*[14] which appears in manuscript as an English sermon reads like a source-book for Latin quotations suitable as authorities. Table Five is a skeleton sermon with a text, the four divisions of the text, headings for subdivisions, and suggested quotations to illustrate each subdivision. No one can imagine a preacher merely listing the eight sins of heart, for example, without any description or illustration. This specimen in the *Speculum* does suggest, however, that the formal characteristics of the 'modern' sermon were available to be imitated by parish priests and not limited to preachers of the court and university circles.

While the formal model of the 'modern' sermon was becoming known to rural priests and the 'old' style undoubtedly still observed, a third kind of organization, probably introduced by friars[15] at first, was rapidly gaining popularity. Mirk's *Festial*[16] is a perfect example of a sermon collection in the vernacular in which almost all the sermons are organized around stories. It was not uncommon for a preacher to use an *exemplum* within a sermon organized according to another style, but in Mirk's compilation we find no formal division and no Biblical exegesis–just stories, linked thinly or not at all. Although such a large group of tales must contain many which were often told before, all the stories are presented without confusion, and some with real talent. Mirk's style is unadorned, except for an occasional metaphor ("For ryght as a knyght sheweth þe wondys þat he haþe yn batayle, yn moche comendyng to hym; ryght so all þe synnys þat a man hath schryuen hym of, and taken hys penans for, schull be þer yschewet yn moch honowre to hym, and moche confucyon to þe fend" [p. 2]), or a bit of vivid depiction ("fendes cryyng, 'Sle, sle, sle, sle, sle, sle, opon þe broche, rost hote, cast ynto þe cawdren, sethe fast yn pyche, and cood, brymston, and hot leed!' " [p. 5]). His sentence structures mainly consist of coordinate clauses, and his diction is of everyday speech rarely compounded with any but the most common theological terms.

The three sermons edited by D. M. Grisdale[17], show an interesting combination of the modern style with heavy emphasis on narrative, and fairly skilful allegorical interpretation of it. Sermon I shows some interest by the preacher in the rhythm of his words, in the use of word pairs ("for-flageld & fobetyn", and "vor-buffet & forbete"), and parallel phrases ("nyth withowten dai, peyne with-owten pyte, dispeir withouten hope & soru withouten ende . . ." [p. 14]). Sermon III conveys highly-wrought emotional effects in its telling of the story of the crucifixion and of a Lollard returned to the fold. Although the preacher complains that some men know "þe fablis o Piramus & Tisbe or Iphis or Pante" as well as the Pater Noster (p. 75), he does not scorn to refer in his sermon to Titus and Vespasian, and the sacrifice of the King of Athens, and liken Christ's body to Orpheus' harp (pp. 68-70).

The sermon Chaucer places in the mouth of his worthy rural parson exhibits another combination of the three sermon styles.[18] The overall organization of the sermon goes along 'modern' lines–three main divisions and a great many subdivisions. But when the parson discusses each of the subpoints, he does so with metaphor and observation as well as authority from the Bible and the Fathers. His language and syntax are much closer to the usage of the 'old' style preachers than to the measured eloquence of the 'moderns'. A man immodestly clothed reminds him of a "she ape in full moon" (1. 424) and the devil's delight in man's lechery to a merchant's pride in the "chaffare that he hath moost advantage of" (1. 850). The rhythms of carefully balanced phrasing and economy of words found in *Middle English Sermons,* No. 39, are replaced in the Parson's Tale by homely wordiness like this: "The cause why that Job clepeth helle the lond of derkness, understandeth that he clepeth it . . ." (1. 180). Just as the three sermons in Grisdale's book combine modern and narrative techniques, Chaucer combines modern organization with the old style.

There is, then, a great deal of diversity in prose techniques among fourteenth-century writers. The mystics convey their special warmth and lyricism in carefully handled rhythms and figures; the translators attain clarity and system without foregoing evidences of personal style. Preachers made use of a variety of approaches, from the formalism of the schools to the naiveté of folk demonology, each according to his estimate of the needs of his hearers. With such a range of possibilities at hand, what Wyclif decided to leave unused, as well as what he adapted, is relevant to the discussion of his style.

[1] J. S. Phillimore, "Blessed Thomas More and the Arrest of Humanism in England", *Dublin Review,* CLIII (1913), p. 8.

[2] See R. W. Chambers, *On the Continuity of English Prose* (*EETS,* OS, 186) (London, 1932), for an extended discussion of the point.

[3] The specimens of Rolle's work selected for close study are those judged to be most free of poetic techniques. They are selections IV, V, VI, VII, and VIII of *English Prose Treatises of Richard Rolle of Hampole,* ed. George G. Perry (*EETS,* OS, 20) (London, 1866).

[4] *The Cloud of Unknowing and the Book of Privy Counselling,* ed. Phyliss Hodgson (*EETS,* OS, 218) (London, 1874-93).

[5] He says ". . . nieþer þou rede it, ne write it, ne speke it . . .", p. 1.

[6] *Revelations of Divine Love,* ed. Grace Warrack (London, 1901). Miss Warrack modernizes punction, diction, and spelling except in cases of "special significance or charm".

[7] *Scala Perfection,* University Microfilms 1403. References are given to chapters because the pages are unnumbered.

[8] The 'university' method is described later in this chapter.

[9] *Mandeville's Travels,* ed. P. Hamelius (*EETS,* OS, 153) (London, 1919).

[10] *Dialogues inter Militem et Clericum,* ed. A. J. Perry (*EETS,* OS, 167) (London, 1925).

[11] A. J. Perry offers a full analysis of these features in his introduction to the volume.

[12] Ed. Woodburn O. Ross (*EETS,* OS, 209) (London, 1940).

[13] See Joseph Albert Mosher, *The Exemplum in the Early Religious and Didactic Literature of England* (New York, 1911).

[14] Ed. G. Holmstedt (*EETS,* OS, 182) (London, 1929). The *Speculum* was apparently a very popular instruction book for parish priests, current from about 1360 into the fifteenth century.

[15] See Mosher, *The Exemplum*, and G. R. Owst, *Preaching in Medieval England* (Cambridge, England, 1926).

[16] Ed. Theodor Erbe (*EETS,* ES, 96) (London, 1905).

[17] *Three Middle English Sermons from the Worchester Manuscript F10,* ed. D. M. Grisdale (*Leeds School of Engl. Lang. Texts and Monographs,* No. 5).

[18] *The Complete Works of Chaucer,* ed. Fred N. Robinson, 2nd ed. (Cambridge, Mass., 1957). References in the text are to lines.

3

THE PURPOSE: WYCLIF'S VIEWS ON PREACHING

There are five distinct groups into which the English sermons may be divided. The Sunday Sermons, one set on the gospels and one on the epistles,[1] are based on the scripture lessons adopted by the Church for each Sunday in the year; the gospel series beginning with the first Sunday after Trinity Sunday and the epistle series with the first Sunday in Advent. These two sets appear in parallel columns in one manuscript, Douce 321, and in the source from which Bodleian 788 was copied, (as the scribe reveals in an interesting error).[2] It is very likely that they were written simultaneously, since Sermon XLVII of the gospel set and XXVII of the epistle set refer to the same proclamation of indulgence by a pope, and the two Sundays on which the sermons should be given are only five weeks apart.[3] Wyclif probably intended one of each set to be preached every Sunday, for he ends the last sermon of the epistle series with, "And þus mai preestis of Cristis secte teche þe puple on Sundaies, boþe þi þe gospel and þe pistle, al$_3$if fals prophetis bigilen hem not" (II, 376).

The thirty-one sermons called 'Common Sanctorum' are based on texts for special feast-days according to the usage of the Sarum missal. They are dedicated to 'an apostle', 'one martyr', and so on, while the thirty-eight 'Proprium Sanctorum' sermons bear the names of specific events, as 'the vigil of St. Andrew', and 'the epiphany'. The latter also follow the order of the Sarum missal, except that they omit the office of Thomas of Canterbury. The Ferial Gospels are for services held on weekdays, 'ferias' being an eccesiastical term for all days except Saturday at first, but gradually coming to exclude Sunday as well. The gospel texts for these one hundred sixteen sermons are those of the Sarum missal.[4]

There is no way of deciding whether Wyclif himself ever preached these sermons. There are some reasons for believing them to have been produced late in his career, after his retirement from Oxford. The opportunity was certainly present, for he was living in his rural parish of Lutterworth, where, it is a matter of record, he died attending to priestly duties. If he did preach these sermons himself, it was unquestionably not in this form. Their contents clearly indicate that he intended them as guides to preachers, perhaps specifically for his band of 'poor priests', to amplify and alter as they saw fit. At the conclusion of Sermon I (I, 3), for example, the reader is told, "þus shulde we warne boþ o man and oþer how sum men shal be dampnyd . . .". In II (I, 6), we read, "Here may men touche all manere of synne . . . and make knowe to þe peple the cautelis of Anticrist", and in III (I, 9), "We may touche in þis gospel what spediþ men and what þing lettiþ men for to be saved . . . ". Later the preacher is told, "Of þis undirstondinge men may take moral witt how men shal lyve, and large þe mater as hem likeþ" (I, 53). Referring to the central metaphor of the text, Wyclif notes "Of þes feveris, and medecyne of hem, may men make a longe speche" (II, 169), and of the twenty-eight conditions of service to God, "Ech of þes pointis þat Paul telliþ mai be alargid to þe puple, and declared diffusely after þat God moveþ þe speker" (II, 271-2).[5]

In his concern that his method should be mastered by other faithful preachers, Wyclif is only participating in a common activity of the Church in his century. In fact the treatises on sermon-making surviving from this period far outnumber the extant sermons themselves. The unusual thing about these skeletal sermons is their peculiar method of stark Bible commentary, as opposed to the formality, heavy allegorization, or story-telling of many others, and the fact that the church year is complete, the lack of such completeness in others giving evidence of a lack of continuous Sunday preaching.[6]

Any prose ought to be judged with reference to its intended audience. In this case the audience consists first of the preachers for whom these sermons will serve as models, and then of the local audiences who will hear the enlarged versions. It is particularly important, therefore, to understand Wyclif's stated aims in preaching. His statements cover a variety of issues, but they interlock to show a closely reasoned view of the subject. It is relevant to consider Wyclif's views on the importance of preaching, its proper subject matter, the use of the vernacular by preachers, the exclusion of all but Biblical material, the emphasis to be placed on allegory, the role of human wisdom, the best methods of organization, and the propriety of discussing contemporary events. In addition, the practice of the orthodox pulpit should be examined on all the same points.

Wyclif considered preaching God's word the most important duty of any priest. The Latin sermons stress this function continually,[7] and its neglect is one of the most often repeated and virulent attacks of the polemical tracts.[8] He is especially bitter about the system of licenses for preachers which, in his opinion, prevented the teaching of the gospel "for jurisdiccioun or oþer cause" (I, 361). He represents prelates as 'gre-houndis' pursuing God's true 'hares' (II, 359). The special ardour with which this point is pressed is accounted for when we recall that Wyclif's followers, many well educated and tonsured priests (at least while Wyclif lived to supervise the movement), were travelling around England preaching and teaching in return for food and lodging from the community. Wyclif must have been dismayed to find that the worst opposition to such preachers came from the hierarchy of the Church.

Although Wyclif teaches that the preacher's personal understanding of the law of Christ must precede active preaching (I, 332), he does not believe the contemplative life enough for a priest. He has only contempt for those who neglect Christ's command and example in preaching and 'gather in wete lumpis' for contemplation while other men 'goo to helle'.[9]

No less important than this message and usually coupled with it, is Wyclif's insistence on what must be preached. Only the message of the gospel is worthy of the preacher's effort and the people's attention (I, 332). The charge against the friars is not that they do not preach, but that they preach falsehood, dreams, or the wisdom of men (I, 176-7, 361; II, 19, 192, 216, 361). Nor does he charge them with being unskillful; on the contrary, they are so good that they seduce the people from their parish priests to listen to their "rymes and gabbings", thus preventing the hearing of the gospel. He even seems to admit their erudition in denouncing their "curiouse preching of Latyn", because it pridefully leads many to "prechen hemsilf, and leeve to preche Jesus Crist", and to neglect the true end of a sermon, "profit to þe soule of þe peple" (II, 19).[10]

The conscientious priest will place the gospels before the people in their own language and in an understandable form, for medicine cures nothing unless it is carefully adapted to the disease (II, 330).[11] The arguments of the schools have no place in these sermons, but simply "practik, put in dede, how men shulde lyve by Goddis law . . . not speculatif, of gemetrie, ne oþer sciencis" (I, 241). Nor do we need to "dreeme" about "newe pointes þat þe gospel leveþ" (I, 13). Therefore, "muse we not", says Wyclif time and again, about the name of Tobies hound (I, 13), how the martyr Zacarie was killed (I, 323), how Jonah got out of the whale (II, 52), what Thomas doubted (II, 140), what country the three kings came from (II, 243), or how many thousands God killed for fornication (II, 334). Such "veyn curiouste were a tempting of God", and a flaw in our belief that "Crist wroot here as myche as was nedeful us to cunne" (II, 88). From this precept Wyclif challenges some of the basic teaching of the church about sin, for according to the Reformer, it is not profitable to distinguish deadly and venial sin, "but ech synne shulde a man flee, lest it be dedli to him" (I, 61).

Nor did Wyclif intend this lesson only for simple folk in rural congregations. The Latin sermons and treatises are filled with the same idea, insisting, even while arguing in the full scholastic format, that unadorned scripture is the only acceptable guide for the church.[12] The authority of the Fathers is perfectly admissible as long as it is considered merely the reflection of wise men on the Bible; in no case may it take precedence over the Bible.[13] Since even Peter was capable of error, by Christ's own words, any other Christian, no matter how wise, is also fallible.[14] The Pope's view on theological matters should not be sought unless he is an especially talented student of Scripture.[15]

The plan in Wyclif's mind was very probably a reorganization of the Church according to scripture rather than canon law. If this is true, the puzzle of the awkward, unidiomatic 'first Wycliffite translation' is largely solved. By this reasoning, Wyclif's plan in the early version was an English 'construe' of the Latin, a word by word rendering which would have full scholarly authority and could, therefore, be accepted all over England as decisive in ecclesiastical matters. The version completed after Wyclif's death, probably by John Purvey, was designed to fill the need for a vernacular Bible to be used devotionally by the people and their priests, and necessarily required a smoother and more idiomatic rendering. This theory explains why Wyclif never used either 'Wycliffite' version when he translated from the Bible—the first was not meant for teaching, but for the government of the Church, and the second did not appear until after his death.[16]

Even these observations, however, do not fully explain Wyclif's stated views of a preacher's duties. Once the Bible is accepted as a supreme authority, there remains the problem of a suitable method of Biblical interpretation. If the words of Scripture were completely self-explanatory, there would be no need for preaching at all. Wyclif maintains that many passages contain several layers of understanding, not all of which are available to every listener. This is his explanation for Christ's use of parables. To unworthy men there will seem to be nothing revealed, but the greater the effort of the worthy man to understand, the more deeply he will be allowed to see. Furthermore, parable is a way of revealing the deep things of the spirit to men untrained in formal philosophy (1, 105). The four levels of Scriptural exegesis are described by Wyclif thus: "Þe first undirstondinge is pleyne, bi letter of þe storye. Þe secounde undirstondinge is clepid witt allegoric, whan men undirstonden bi witt of þe lettre, what þing shal falle here bifore þe dai of dome. Þe þridde undirstondinge is clepid tropologik, and it techiþ how men shulden lyve here in vertues. Þe fourþe undirstondinge is clepid anagogike, and it telliþ how it shal be wiþ men þat ben in hevene" (I, 30; also II, 277-78), but he rarely finds it necessary to discuss all four levels in connection with the same text. He has, in fact, a rather sensible view of the extent of Scriptural allegory: "For sym þing is seid in figure, and sum þing bi his owne kynde . . ." (II, 375), and "treuþis þat ben more nedeful ben writun þere more expresly" (II, 225). Wyclif's scorn is not directed against allegory in the interpretation of Scripture, as Owst suggests,[17] but against the avoidance of the implications of a literal understanding: "Þes wordis of Crist ben scorned of gramariens and devynes. Gramariens and filosophris seien, þat Crist knewe not his gendris; and bastard dyvynes seien algatis þat þes wordis of Crist ben false, and so no wordis of Crist bynden, but to þe witt þat gloseris tellen" (I, 376), and "here Anticristis tirauntis speken a$_3$en þe newe lawe, and seien þat literal witt of it shulde nevere be taken, but goostli witt; and þei feynen þis goostli witt after shrewid wille þat þei han" (II, 343). In this insistence on the obligation of the interpreter to account for the literal level of the text even while he is explaining its other implications, Wyclif is clinging to a patristic method now often called typological rather than allegorical.[18]

One of the serious charges against later generations of Lollards is that they lacked respect for the mysteries of religion and placed their own common sense above centuries of attempts to communicate that which is finally ineffable.[19] Some, by no means all, of the Lollard abjurations in the early fifteenth century do reveal a certain literal-mindedness which one feels inappropriate to religious devotion. Wyclif himself was heartily against any such reliance on human powers. In the English sermons he speaks of the pitiful state of our knowledge of God: "þis shulen we fulli knowun in hevene, but here we blabren it as blynd men" (II, 355; see also II, 224), and of the inadequacy of words to reveal the believing heart: "but sum glymerynge we have in oure soule of þis treuþe, and betere knowen it in oure herte þan we can speke it in vois" (I, 127).

The Latin treatises bear no message so consistently as that of the unfathomable nature of God. But where some schoolmen, following William of Occam, had taken this point of departure for their divorce between theology and philosophy, and their consequent speculative freedom in philosophy, Wyclif returns to the conservative position of realism, even to the extent of denying validity to philosophy when its conclusions could not be reconciled with revealed dogma. Wyclif displays a marked reverence for the opinions of Bradwardine, the latter-day champion of realism, and shares his scorn for the nominalists whom he, like Bradwardine, labels Pelagians.[20] The real charge, one sees, against Pelagians is not so much that they are wrong (although he believes they are) but that they trust excessively in the capacities of their own minds. It is ironic that later generations have enshrined Wyclif's name as the defender of free thought, when of all the fourteenth-century schoolmen he and Bradwardine are certainly the most mistrustful of human wisdom.

Yet from another point of view the charge against Wyclif is justified. Although he placed no faith in the mind of unregenerate man, he did exercise reason with unusual freedom when he believed he had direct Biblical evidence for his position, and he seemed to urge that other men should do likewise (" . . . omnis homo debet esse theologus"[21]). In the hands of a trained scholar and sensitive believer, independent thought and spiritual insight can surely coexist. But after the first generation of Lollards there was bound to be a deterioration of one faculty or the other. Wyclif, fortunately or unfortunately, left vigorous thought as his legacy, just as Rolle had left poetic insight.

On the proper organization for a sermon, Wyclif makes his views clear. Although his Latin sermons pay due obeisance to the practices of scholastic debate, such techniques he believes to be unnecessary and inappropriate for vernacular sermons to lay people. The plain text, explained sentence by sentence, is the best plan of attack, suiting the depth of the discussion to the ability of the hearers: "... it is not profitable to preche unto rude men subtilite of þe Trinite, or oþir þat þei cunnen not conseyve" (II, 330). And again, "And þus bi autorite of þe lawe of God men shulden speke her wordis as Goddis lawe spekiþ, and strange not in speche from undirstondinge of þe puple ..." (I, 78-79). Important as it is, the didactic purpose does not submerge the inspirational–"þis sentence shulde move men to be martiris for love of Crist" (II, 325).

Not only should the people be taught what the Scripture means, but also what relevance it has to their lives and society. It is this consideration that moves Wyclif to the invective he directs against the practice of religion in his own day. In several passages he points out that the rebuking of errors is, according to the Bible, an essential part of preaching. In fact, he cites silence in cases which require Godly indignation as acquiescence in the sin itself (II, 201-2). Thus the simple setting-forth of 'Goddis lawe' really has two parts–presenting and clarifying the texts themselves, and applying the precepts which emerge to contemporary matters.

More difficult than ascertaining Wyclif's ideas about preaching is examining what the rest of the fourteenth-century Church thought. It soon became a standard charge against Lollards that they exalted the function of preaching to the point of neglecting the sacraments; yet men of the solidly orthodox party of the Church, exactly contemporary with Wyclif, show as much concern, sometimes in much the same terms as the Reformer, over the clergy's general neglect of preaching, ignorance of basic Scriptural materials, and disposition to please rich hearers rather than to instruct them.[22]

If we consider the preaching duties of the local curate, excluding for a moment the activities of monks and friars, there will be little question that regular Sunday preaching was not the case in all parishes. The Constitutions of Archbishop Peckham, appearing in 1281, required a sermon from every priest four times a year, and yet a full century after that decree Bishop Thoresby complained that few of the common people knew even their Paternoster, Ave, or Creed.[23] Before giving full credence to such statements, we must remember the exaggeration which is likely to accompany a prelate's rebukes to those under his charge, and the extremely forthright character of self-criticism within the ranks of the clergy.[24] It was not until the taint of Lollardy began to be attached to such attempts at reform that they faded into the background and, early in the fifteenth century, died out among the orthodox. While Wyclif was writing, the ideal of a clergy preaching vigorously and regularly was very much alive, however scarce compliance with the ideal might have been.

Even Cardinal Gasquet, who in 1897 revived the two-century old controversy over the prevalence of pre-Reformation preaching in the hope of proving the competence of the clergy, had to admit that much religious instruction was carried on through institutions other than the sermon, as a sort of catechetical training.[25] B. L. Manning believes that individual teaching and admonition was given through the confessional, reducing the burden the sermon had to carry.[26] Even so, interest in good preaching was running high among the orthodox.

There is no mistaking the direction of contemporary evidence about mendicant preaching and the bitterness it caused between friars and parish priests. The friars were good at drawing audiences, good at holding attention and good at begging at the end of the sermon. All this undoubtedly lowered the local priest's revenues and prestige. When the friars first came to England, inspired with their mission of teaching and helping the poor, their competition must have raised preaching standards, for Dominicans especially were noted for their learning. By the late fourteenth century, however, the movement had subsided into an institution, and the practice of preaching largely into a money-getting technique.[27]

The very large numbers of extant sermon manuals dating from this period adds weight to the conclusion that the preaching office was neglected or abused, but at the same time it indicates that the hierarchy was worried about the matter. Some of the very men who sat as Wyclif's judges at his trials for heresy authored sermons and directives no less strongly-worded or strongly-conceived than the charges of the Reformer himself.[28] The difference is that the bishops preached to the clergy and composed (or at least preserved) their sermons in Latin.[29] There is not, as in Wyclif, the direct appeal to the people to correct their priests' lives as well as their own, or to the nobility to use the weapon of property against an irresponsible clergy.

The attitude of the Church toward vernacular preaching was clearly favorable. Peckham's Constitutions specifically urged vernacular sermons on the basic doctrines of the faith to be preached four times a year. Often, no doubt, the local curate conscientiously complied. Thoresby urged his readers to "here godys lawe taw$_3$t in þy modyr tonge".[30] We can hardly expect to find great numbers of these sermons surviving; the priest may have made only rough notes for himself, but even if he wrote brilliantly he would find himself unable to incur the expense of publishing his manuscripts. The hierarchy placed only two restrictions on his efforts: he must not discuss subtle questions of doctrine or arouse anti-clerical sentiment among the people.

On the sufficiency of the Bible as a guide for living, there is a clear cleavage between Wyclif and his contemporaries, in both theory and practice. There was at this time probably no settled dogma concerning the infallibility of the Scriptures,[31] and certainly nothing to indicate their *exclusive* authority. Quotations from the Latin Fathers and debates structured like those of the schoolmen rivalled the Bible in the sermons of the moderately learned. On the more popular side, there were innumerable fables and chronicles which could be turned to edifying attention-holders. While one group of sermon-treatises specifically condemns both affectations of learning and obscuring of Scripture by *exempla*,[32] the great majority of guides for preachers specifically recommend them. John de Bromyard found it necessary to index his one thousand *exempla* in one hundred eighty nine categories for his readers' convenience.[33] With Mirk's famous *Festial* "the text of canonical scriptures would seem almost out of favour",[34] crowded out by saints' legends so incredible as scarcely to do more than baptise certain pagan superstitions with new, holy names. No wonder Owst calls Wyclif's insistence on the sufficiency of the Scriptures his great contribution.

If more evidence for the acquiescence of the Church in allegorical interpretation of Scripture were required than the rich tradition of sermon and devotional literature immediately supplies, it can be found in the explicit statements of Master Rypon of Durham.[35] Rypon uses the allegorical method himself, but he goes on to explain the four-fold sense of Scripture in some detail, and to show why Biblical literalism caused both Lollards and Mendicants (Rypon himself was a Benedictine) to fall into heresy.[36] The controversy was apparently very widely known, for Chaucer expected his readers to understand the summoner's remark "For lettre sleeth, so as we clerkes seyn".[37]

This privilege of non-literal interpretation belonged, of course, to the clergy. A great deal of speculative freedom was allowed the higher clergy, as witnessed by the approval with which the Church viewed Peacock's work in the early stages of his career, even while he was advocating an extreme form of rationalism which asserted the superiority of syllogism over Biblical authority. A similar trust in the powers of the simple layman is altogether absent, and even the mystics, whose direct communication with God might lead them to say otherwise, warn their readers against any offense against the Holy Church. The very edict which Archbishop Peckham directed toward the religious education of the laity exhibits distrust of their hearing the Scriptures themselves. What should be taught in the vernacular is "the Creed, the Ten Commandments, the two precepts of the Gospel, vis. love to God and man, the seven works of mercy, the seven deadly sins, the seven cardinal virtues and the seven sacraments of grace". For lay people these *are* the fundamentals of the faith.

Although Wyclif and his men were not completely alone in seeking to organize their sermons around simple explanation and interpretation of the text, they were unquestionably a minority voice. The normal sermon, as the priest was advised to design it, followed a rather set form. A theme was declared, and 'ante-theme' prayer offered, the theme repeated, introduced, and then divided into three or more sub-themes. The theme might be chosen from the gospel for the day, the epistle, the lesson, or even from non-Biblical materials. The ante-theme asks God's blessing on the preacher so that he may move hearts. Thomas Walleys, aware of the difficulty of introducing the theme, offers three methods–authority, *exemplum,* and natural reason. Divisions in the text might be made by observing the species of virtues and vices involved, by noting the various characteristics of some important symbol in the text, or by finding 'questions' related to the theme. A simple conclusion summarized and completed the sermon.[38] This method perhaps somewhat simplified for use in rural pulpits, competed for primacy with a method based on *exempla.*

Wyclif was not alone in sanctioning the use of invective in the pulpit. As we have already seen, the higher clergy made excellent use of it in preaching to the lower, and the monks in their days of reform spirit caused even prelates to tremble. The friars began their work in England by establishing a tradition of free-spoken criticism of every class, inside and outside the Church 'before all the people'.[39] Although that golden age was over, the tradition was begun, and the terms of abuse of the high clergy by Spiritual Franciscans ('whore of Babylon', 'antichrist', etc.) lingered in lay ears until a generation or so before Wyclif made them ring openly again.

Only one element of Wyclif's views on preaching, then, can be seen as a thoroughly new concept in the Church–the sufficiency of the Bible. Some element in the orthodox church had already declared its sympathy with Wyclif's other tenets: the importance of preaching, the necessity for using English, the possibility of allegorical interpretation, the organization based on line-by-line explanation, and the inclusion of topical criticism. Wyclif's remorseless logic led him to unite these extant elements, ordering them in terms of his view of the Bible and shaping them into a weapon against the 'modern' practices which he felt to be so far from Christ's ideals. How successfully he himself would be able to fulfill his own conditions is, in one sense, my real subject.

[1] The Sunday Gospels are found in Arnold's edition of *Select English Works* (London, 1869), I, 1-162. The Sunday Epistles are in volume II, 221-376.

[2] Introduction to *Select English Works,* XIII, n. 1.

[3] See volume I, 137 and volume II, 302 of *Select English Works.*

[4] The Comoun Sanctorum and Proprium Sanctorum sermons are in volume I, 165-412, the Ferial Gospel sermons in volume II, 1-217.

[5] I know of only one reader of the sermons who does not acknowledge this function of the sermons. E. W. Talbert says "In a group of sermons meant for use throughout the church year in the performance of the liturgy and composed in an age of wooden sermonizing, there is no need to explain the presence of such 'directions'... by suggesting that the sermons were not orally delivered". "The Date of the Composition of

the English Wycliffite Collection of Sermons", *Speculum,* XII (Oct. 1937), 464-474. There is too much emphasis in the directions on the distinction between priest and people, to take the passages as simply indications of Lollard hermeneutical precepts, as Talbert suggests we should.

[6] G. R. Owst, *Preaching in Medieval England* (Cambridge, England, 1926), p. 235.

[7] *Sermones,* ed. Johann Loserth (Wyclif Society; London, 1890), pp. 16, 22, 34, 248, are just a few cases.

[8] *Polemical Works in Latin, Latin Works,* I, ed. Rudolf Buddensieg (Wyclif Society; London, 1883) Part I, 20, 117-119, 126; Part II, 425, 492, etc.

[9] F. D. Matthew, ed., *English Works Hitherto Unprinted* (*EETS*, OS, 74) (London, 1880), p. 187.

[10] *De Officio Regis, Latin Works,* VIII, ed. A. W. Pollard and C. Sayle (Wyclif Society; London, 1887), p. XVII makes the same point.

[11] The metaphor occurs in the passage cited in the text. Other, more specific, confirmations of Wyclif's belief in vernacular preaching are found in I, 129, 209; II, 221; in numerous tracts of Lollard authorship; and in the Latin works.

[12] *De Officio Regis,* 111.

[13] *De Apostasia, Latin Works,* IX, ed. M. H. Dziewickie (Wyclif Society: London, 1889), p. 113. The whole tract "Veritate Sacre Scriptura" printed as Arnold's No. XII in vol. III of the *Select English Works* carries this message. The Latin text is not printed.

[14] *De Ecclesia, Latin Works,* IV, ed. J. Loserth (Wyclif Society; London, 1886), p. 507.

[15] *De Apostasia,* p. 173.

[16] See Margaret Deanesley, *The Significance of the Lollard Bible* (London, 1951), pp. 5-8.

[17] G. R. Owst, *Literature and the Pulpit* (Cambridge, England, 1933), pp. 61-62.

[18] See Charles Donahue "Patristic Exegesis: the Summation", *Critical Approaches to Medieval Literature, English Institute Essays,* 1960 (New York, 1961).

[19] See James Gairdner, C. B., *Lollardy and the Reformation in England* (London, 1908), I, 1-86.

[20] See Gordon Leff, *Bradwardine and the Pelagians, Cambridge Studies in Medieval Life and Thought* (Cambridge, England, 1957), for Bradwardine's view.

[21] *De Civili Domino, Latin Works,* II, ed. R. L. Poole and J. Loserth (Wyclif Society; London, 1885-1900), I, 402.

[22] Owst, *Preaching,* p. 46.

[23] *Lay Folks Catechism,* ed. T. F. Simmons and H. E. Nolloth (*EETS,* 18) (London, 1901), p. 4.

[24] "The candour and capacity for criticism among preachers and writers of this period is remarkable. The one failing that cannot be charged against the fourteenth-century English Church is that of complacency". W. A. Pantin, *The English Church in the Fourteenth Century* (Cambridge, England, 1955), p. 238.

[25] *The Old English Bible and Other Essays* (London, 1897).

[26] *The People's Faith in the Time of Wyclif* (Cambridge, England, 1919), p. 29.

[27] Owst in *Preaching* (pp. 85-89) draws this conclusion from the evidence provided not only by Lollards and satirists (Chaucer and Langland), but from the friars' own charges against members of their orders.

[28] Bishop Brunton and John de Bromyard, for example. Owst, *Preaching,* pp. 15-20 and *Literature,* p. 251. William de Rymyngton, S. T. P., author of several treatises against Wyclif, himself painted "the darkest account of the Church and some of the fiercest denunciation of fellow clergy to be found in all English sermon literature". Owst, *Literature*, p. 273.

[29] Owst, *Preaching,* p. 224.

[30] *Lay Folks Catechism,* p. 41.

[31] See James Gairdner, C. B., *Lollardy and the Reformation,* vol. I, book I, ch. III.

[32] This is a very interesting group of vernacular writings from the north of England, scarcely separable from Lollard writings in technique, although strongly anti-Lollard in sentiment. See Owst, *Preaching,* pp. 239-240.

[33] Owst, *Preaching,* p. 303.
[34] Owst, *Preaching,* p. 245.
[35] For the tradition see Beryl Smalley's, *The Study of the Bible in the Middle Ages* (New York, 1952).
[36] The sermon is outlined in Owst, *Literature,* pp. 58-62; it is not yet in print.
[37] *Summoners Tale*, 1, 1794.
[38] Owst and Woodburn O. Ross, editor of the EETS printing of *Middle English Sermons,* agree on this format for the learned sermon. A very close adherence to this outline is seen in Number 39 of *Middle English Sermons,* discussed in Chapter II, above.
[39] For the influence of both monks and friars see Owst, *Preaching*, Ch. II.

4

THE TRANSLATIONS: THE SERMON TEXTS AND THE WYCLIFFITE BIBLE

In *The Lollard Bible* Margaret Deanesly clears away the myth surrounding the two complete English translations of the Bible connected with John Wyclif's name.[1] She refutes the earlier view that Wyclif himself had translated both versions and most modern scholars accept her view that he, in fact, produced neither, although Sven Fristedt conjectures a lost revision of the earlier version by Wyclif's own hand.[2] The principle mysteries surrounding the translations – whether there were Middle English versions of the whole Bible before 1383, who actually did the work of translation, and what purposes were to be served by the project–can be discussed with reasonable confidence.

It is never possible to base a firm conclusion on negative evidence alone, especially when the hazards to the survival of a medieval manuscript are considered. But the fact that there are no copies of a complete Middle English Bible translation, no references to one, and no citations of one from those who wished to establish a precedent for their own work or their arguments,[3] leaves the burden of proof to those who claim that such a translation did exist. The only early claim comes from Sir Thomas More, who is now believed to have mistaken a Wycliffite text without the Lollard introduction for an authorized Catholic version.[4] Furthermore, the need for a vernacular version does not seem to have been recognized by the Church, for in none of the very numerous and detailed treatises on the Christian life which we receive from this period is the duty of Bible-reading even suggested to the layman. The Wycliffite versions were never charged with translating inaccurately, but merely with making the Bible, "Common and open to laymen, and women who are able to read".[5] A jest about Oldcastle and part of the charge of heresy against him was that he read the Bible instead of behaving like a knight.[6] Together these considerations create at least suspicion that there were no full translations before 1383, and that if there were, the Wycliffite translations retain the novelty of having been the first designed for publication.[7] It seems safe to say that no complete vernacular version was widely available before Wyclif and that the Church did not encourage the making of one.

Modern opinion, although divided about the authorship of the two translations called Lollard unanimously disclaims anything but an editorial and inspirational function for Wyclif himself. There is excellent evidence for Hereford's participation in the early translation of the Old Testament, and fairly firm reason for believing Purvey to have overseen the production of the later version.[8] Fristedt postulated a third attempt, a revision of the early version, edited by Wyclif himself, but if it ever existed, it is now lost.[9] There are several modern writers who suggest John Trevisa as the author of the later version, but the only testimony comes from Caxton, and some interesting, but inconclusive circumstantial evidence.[10] The later version was almost certainly completed twelve or so years after Wyclif's death, but he may have supervised or encouraged its undertaking, and Purvey would have been the likeliest person to have been entrusted with his friend's project.

Wyclif's belief in the sufficiency of the Bible and his wish to reproduce the New Testament Church in the fourteenth century necessitated an English Bible. He saw that while theology in his day still rested on Scriptural authority, "the enforcement of the Church's jurisdiction rested on canon law".[11] Designing, in a way typical of him, to attack the source of the abuses he saw around him, Wyclif conceived the very large objective of replacing canon law with a vernacular Bible. In addition to a reformation of the organization of the Church, the demand for a return to New Testament Christianity required that an understandable text of the whole Bible be made available to the people. Why these two aims could not be met in a single translation lies in an explanation of the principles of the translation of scripture in medieval times.

For the purposes of scholarly debate, and for the bases of Church organization, there was only one method for Bible translation uniformly found acceptable before the sixteenth century. W. Schwartz writes that "the method of word-for-word translation was considered to be the surest safeguard against any alteration of the original thought. It was considered to render the contents of the Bible in its entirety without any mistakes, and to protect the translator from a change of God's word and from heresy".[12] Such an approach to translation was called 'construe' and was advocated, according to Miss Deanesly, by "the strictest school of translators".[13] Only such a method, then, would suffice for Wyclif's plan to reform Church organization. Rather than mere ineptitude in the English idiom, as was formerly believed, the literalness of the early version may have been part of a careful plan to meet the most rigid specifications for an English Bible.

The second version is not a construe. It was designed to carry out the second part of Wyclif's plan-making vernacular Scripture available to the local priests and to the people. Without hope of settling the vexed question of the Biblical education of the medieval clergy, it may be safely remarked that almost no rural curate could have owned a full Bible, either in Latin or

English, before 1383.[14] Among the higher clergy, ownership of the Bible was probably limited to bishops and extensive knowledge of it to graduates in theology.[15] The later version, then, may have been offered as a basis for the sermons of less well educated priests and a devotional book for literate layman. Purvey's *General Prologue* to this version sets out the principles of his translation, which was intended to render the sentence "as opyn (either opener) in Englyshe as in latyne, and not go far fro the letter". But if the specific words or constructions of the Latin obscure meaning in English, "the wordis owen to serve to ye entente and sentence: and elles the wordis bene superfluouse either false".[16] Henry Hargreaves in his discussion of English Bibles beginning with Bede, concludes that Purvey, "typical of early translators as a group, reaches the highest level of attainment . . . . He accepts that the text needs interpretive aids, but stresses the pre-eminence of the literal meaning and handles his sources with scholarly care".[17]

The texts for the English sermons are almost certainly the only examples of Wyclif's ability as a translator which remain to us.[18] It is from them alone that we may test such statements as: "Wycliffe does not think what language he is supposed to be writing",[19] and, "if he [Wyclif] is over-shadowed by the Latin, his English becomes helpless in the presence of that great competitor".[20] An account of all the divergences between the early and late Bible translations of Matthew and the sermon texts from that book seemed a useful way to conduct a comparison. The texts from Matthew are scattered throughout four of the five sermon groups (the Sunday Epistles are, of course, not represented), and there is no reason to believe that they are not typical of Wyclif's style as a translator.

Of the 196 instances of divergence in diction:

EV and LV are the same 137 times
EV and W are the same 17 times
LV and W are the same 11 times
All three translations are different 31 times

These figures strongly suggest that Wyclif had neither version before him as he rendered his texts; the use of the later version is an historical impossibility, and the choices Wyclif made in common with the early version are only slightly more numerous than those which coincide with the later and may reasonably be attributed to the operation of chance among limited possibilities. The two Wycliffite translations are overwhelmingly closer to each other in diction than either of them is to Wyclif's sermon texts. Many of the differences simply represent the substitution of one common term for another: *walkynge* (EV), *walkide* (LV), *wandrid* (W); *see* (E and LV), *watir* (W); *sendynge* (EV), *castynge* (LV), *putting* (W). A few of the variations involve interpretation: *litil men* (EV), *litle children* (LV), *meke men* (W);

techere of the lawe (E and LV), *doctour of lawe* (W); *presedent* (EV), *iustice* (LV), *Pilat* (W). Some terms Wyclif always translates differently from the Bible versions: *kyngdom* (E and LV), *rewme* (W); *treuli* (E and LV), *soþli* (W); *generacioun* (E and LV), *kynrede* (W); and *worschipide* (E and LV), *lowtide* (W). A few terms are given differently in different passages: *deuelis* (E and LV), *fendis* (W) in Matt. IX, 34, but *feend* (E and LV), *devyl* (W) in Matt. XIII, 39; *leprous* (E and LV) *mesel* (W) in Matt. VIII, 2, but *mesels* (E and LV), and *leprouse men* (W) in Matt. X, 8; and *war* (EV), *sliȝ* (LV), *prudent* (W) in Matt. X, 16, but *prudent* (E and LV), *war* (W) in Matt. XXV, 2.

The most impressive fact, however, which this word count reveals is that when there are different readings EV uses an Old English word as opposed to one of romance origin fifty percent of the time, LV fifty-two percent, and W sixty-six percent. I consider this strong evidence for the consistency of Wyclif's attempts to keep his translations open and homely. It may be argued that innumerable words of romance origin are perfectly integrated with native words in the vocabulary of Englishmen of the late fourteenth century. Yet in tone, if not intelligibility, we must find *tolden afer* (W) more colloquial than *prophecieden* (E and LV), *bad* (W) than *comaundide* (W and LV), *loris* (W) than *doctrines* (E and LV), *takiþ* (W) than *resseyueth* (E and LV), *snybbe* (W) than *repreue* (E and LV), *þe last making of man* (W) than *regeneracioun* (E and LV), *aȝen-biyng* (W) than *redempcioun* (E and LV), *woundirful* (W) than *merueilous* (E and LV), *chaffarynge* (W) than *marchaundise* (E and LV), *put to be upon* (W) than *ordeyned* (E and LV), *maden . . . fair* (W) than *anourneden* (EV) or *araieden* (LV), *han* (W) than *weld* (EV) or *take in possessioun* (LV), *Wende* (W) than *Departe* (E and LV), or *hyed* (W) than *enhaunsid* (E and LV). Nor can we explain the differences by noting historical changes in patterns of usage, for Wyclif's translations are usually dated between those of the two full Bible versions.

Further examples from the translation of other New Testament books yield similar results. The *Oxford English Dictionary* lists no earlier occurrences for *salutatioun* than EV, although there are two (Chaucer and Trevisa) which are contemporary, while *gretyng* (LV and W) is an Old English word, found in 900. EV had *evangelize,* a new word in English (although *evangelist* is found from the twelfth century on and *evangel* is in Rolle's Psalter), where LV has *preche* and W *telle,* both very common Middle English words. LV and the sermons both avoid using *interpretid,* which does occur in Middle English, but is still relatively rare. Both the full versions mention *superflu feestis,* which provides a distinct contrast to *ofte etyngis* in the sermon texts.

In rendering possessives, Wyclif almost invariably substitutes an -es, -is, or -s for the paraphrastic construction. Because the language of the Authorized Version is so familiar to us, expressions like *wymmens children* for *children of wymmen* (E and LV) and *Zebedes sones* (W) for *sones of Zebedee* sound a little un-Biblical, but they attest, like so many of Wyclif's constructions, to a tendency to choose homely phrasings.

In his *General Prologue* to the second version, Purvey was very specific about his treatment of Latin participles as finite English verbs̃, correcting a primary reason for the charges against the first version that it sounds un-English. Indeed the result of a direct substitution of an English participle for a Latin one often gives an unidiomatic reading: "han stolen him, vs slepinge" (EV), which the later version and the sermon texts remedy: "han stolen hym, while 3e slepten" (LV), and "han stolen his bodi while 3e sleepten" (W). But at other times the participle preserves a sophistication and economy of style which is lost in Purvey's string of finite verbs: "And he holdynge forth his hond in to his diciples, seide . . ." (EV), "And he helde forth his hoond in to hise disciplis, and seide . . ." (LV), in which cases Wyclif keeps the participle: "And Crist, stretching his honde to his disciplis, seide . . ." (W). There are also times when Wyclif gives the structure in a clause:

> "his disciplis, hungrynge, bigunnen . . ." (EV)
> "his disciplis hungriden, and bigunnen . . ." (LV)
> "his disciplis, for þei hungriden, begunnen . . ." (W),

in a participial phrase:

> "Sum man was rich, and was clothid in purpur" (EV)
> "There was a riche man, and was clothid in purpur" (LV)
> "Þere was a riche man, cloþid in purpur" (W),

in a prepositional phrase:

> "he, ioyinge puttith on his shuldris" (EV)
> "he ioieth, and leyith it on hise schuldris" (LV)
> "wolde lein it on hise shuldris wiþ joie" (W),

or in a sustantivc:

> "all sellynge and byinge" (EV)
> "alle that bou3ten and solden" (LV)
> "alle bieris and selleris" (W).

The translator of EV predictably uses English participles to translate Latin participles; Purvey, equally predictably, finite verbs; Wyclif ranges freely among the options, making far greater use of the resources of idiomatic English.

Another major difference in phrasing between Wyclif's texts and the full versions of the Bible results from the preacher's habit of imbedding the Scripture in his own sentences, making explanatory remarks between the phrases of his text and often changing direct quotations to indirect ones. Wyclif gives E and LV "keperis" as "knyȝttis þat kepten þe sepulcre", and the direct quotation, "What semeth to ȝou of Crist" (E and LV), as "what hem þouȝt of þe kynde of Crist", continuing the sentence the preacher himself began. Sometimes this practice produces a smoother, briefer phrasing:

> "axide hise disciplis, and seide [seyinge-EV], Whom seien men to be mannus sone?" (E and LV)
> "axide what men seide of him" (W),

and:

> "and seide (sayings-EV), ȝelde that that thou owest" (E and LV)
> "and bade him paie his dette" (W).

Sometimes this practice leads to an interpretation of the text rather than a close translation: "Chirche", for vineyard in the parable about hiring laborers, "enemy to Crist", for the enemy of the parable of the tares, and "preie ȝe God to move his prechours" where the literal text gives the terms of the parable of the ripe corn, "preye ȝe the lord of the ripe corn, that he sende worke men in to his ripe corn" (E and LV).

In still other passages, Wyclif shows a tendency to summarize items in the text:

(1) "Where nether ruste ne mouȝte distrieth, and where theues deluen not out, ne stelen" (E and LV)
"where noon of þes four þingis fallen" (W),

(2) "Abraham and Ysaac and Jacob" (E and LV)
"patriarkes" (W),

(3) "hauynge tweyne hoondis or twey feet to be sent in to euerlastynge fier" (E and LV)
"þan to have here þes lymes and after be sent to helle" (W).

An extended example of this technique is found in the reading of Matthew XXV, 31:

> "whanne siȝen we thee hungry, and we fedden thee; thristi, and we ȝauen to thee drynk? and whanne sayne we thee herborles, and we herboreden thee; or nakid and we hiliden thee? or whanne sayn we thee sijk, or in prisoun, and we camen to thee?" (E and LV)

"when sawe we þee in þese statis, hungry, or þirsti, herboreles, or nakid in bodi, syke or in prisoun, and we diden þus to þee, Lord?" (W)

Obviously, only a certain kind of Scriptural passage provides the right context for this sort of streamlining, and some might say that part of the rhythm of these passages disappears under Wyclif's pen, but a close look reveals another rhythm being created, characterized by the preacher's clarity and conciseness.

Wyclif's translations consistently economize:

(1) "thei that ben of clene herte" (E and LV)
"men of clene herte" (W),

(2) "To no thing it is worth ouere, no but that it be cast [sent-LV] out" (E and LV)
"þis salt is not worþ after but to be casten out" (W),

(3) "is sente in to the fournyse" (EV)
"is cast in to an ouen" (LV)
"is brent" (W),

(4) "scheep not hauynge a scheepherde" (E and LV)
"sheep wiþouten herde" (W),

(5) "But the cumpanyes that wenten before, and that sueden, crieden, seyinge . . ." (EV)
"And the puple that wente bifore, and that sueden, crieden, and seiden . . ." (LV)
"and oþir, comynge bifore and bihynde songen . . ." (W),

(6) "that it shulde be fulfillid, that thing that is seid by the prophete, seyinge . . ." (EV)
"that it shulde be fulfillid, that is seid bi the prophete, seiynge . . ." (LV)
"to fulfille þat word þat was spoken of þe prophete" (W),

(7) "foldid on knees byfore hym, seyinge . . ." (EV)
"feide doun on hise knees bifore hym, and seide . . ." (LV)
"knelyng bifore him, and seide . . ." (W).

Wyclif rarely expands a phrasing unless he adds explanatory details; his telescoping seems to result in more idiomatic English, even to the really homely "þes two folk saten upon Moises chaier", where E and LV have "On the chayere of Moises, scribes and Parisees han sete".

Many of Wyclif's passages are clearer than the readings given by either of the versions of the whole Bible. "Biheestis of fadris" (E and LV), becomes "Behestis þat weren maad to fadris" (W); and "the tyme determyned of the fadir" (LV), becomes "þe tyme þat his fadir wole þat he be tretid as lord" (W). The full versions render Matthew XIII, 49: "and schulen departe yvel men fro the myddil of iuste men. And thei shulen sende him in to the chymnei of fier", but Wyclif writes, "and shal departe yvel men fro juste men, and shal sende yvel men in to þe chymeney of fier". Here are two explanations of what happened to the food Christ ate after his resurrection: "and is sent out in to the goyng awei" (E and LV), "and is sent out as departid filþe" (W). The two versions of the Bible have "Lord, if thou art, comaunde us", where Wyclif has "Lord, if þou be Crist, comand me". At least once Wyclif's translation represents the Vulgate more faithfully:

> "sciotote quia me priorem vobis odio habuit" (Vulgate)
> "wite ȝe, for it hadde me in hate first than ȝou" (EV)
> "wite ȝe, that it had me in hate rather than ȝou" (LV)
> "ȝe shulden wele wite þat it hatid me bifore" (W).

Very often Wyclif offers readings which seem more impressive in emphasis and rhythm than the same passages in the early and later versions. Emphasis is better managed in: "Him þat Moises haþ writun in þe lawe and prophetis, we han founden, Jesus, Josepis sone, of Nazareþ" (W), than in "We han founden Jhesus the sone of Joseph, of Nazareth whom Moyses wroot in the lawe and profetis" (E and LV), in "Crist went in to þe hous, and toke þe hand of þe wenche, and saide, Wench, rys up. And þe wenche roos" (W), than in "he entride in, and held hir honde; and the wenche roos vp" (EV), or "he wente in, and helde hir hond; and the damysel roos" (LV), in "Jesus shulde save his peple fro þer synnes" (W), than in "he schal make his people saaf fro her synnes" (E and LV). The rhythm is more appealing in "eeren to heere" (W), than in "eris of heryng" (E and LV), in "See þat þou telle no man" (W), than in "Se, seie thou to no man" (E and LV), in "What dreden ȝe of litil feiþ" (W), than in "What ben ȝe of litil feith agaste?" (E and LV), and in "and þei weren restid anoon" (W), than in "a greet pesibilnesse was maad" (E and LV). Sometimes Wyclif's phrases exhibit a rather graceful parallelism: "ȝe token freely, þerfore ȝyve freeli" as opposed to "freeli ȝe han takun, freli ȝyue ȝe" (E and LV), and "þat yvel kynrede and kynrede of hoordoom" (W), as opposed to "an yuel generacioun and auoutere" (EV), and "An yuel kynrede and a spouse brekere" (LV). Sometimes these rhythms give a sense of conclusion: "and þei diden also to hem" (W), as opposed to "in lijk maner thei diden to hem" (E and LV), "he þat lastiþ to þe eende" (W), as opposed to "he that schal dwelle stable in to (Unto-EV) the ende" (E and LV), and "to þe end of þe world" (W), as opposed to "til the endyng of the world" (EV), and "in to the ende of the world" (LV).

What all this means, I think, is that John Wyclif took his duties as a Bible translator very seriously. If personal piety and social order must be nourished by constant study of "Goddis word", Wyclif was willing to make an understandable text of it available to Englishmen, usually in language more flexible, economical, idiomatic, unambiguous, emphatic, and rhythmic than any translator before him, or after, for that matter, until Tyndale. Wyclif does think what language he is writing, nor is his style overshadowed by what most commentators describe as the thoroughly decadent Latin of the fourteenth-century schools.

[1] *Cambridge Studies in Medieval Life and Thought* (Oxford, 1920).
[2] *The Wycliffite Bible, Stockholm Studies in English,* IV (Stockholm, 1953).
[3] Purvey, for example, would like to have established a precedent for his translation by citing similar earlier attempts. In his tract of 1405, he is only able to adduce partial versions or catechisms like Gaytrik's, nor are his contemporary opponents able to cite anything since Bede. Trevisa, too, would have used precedents to strengthen his case for English prose translations in *Dialogue between A Lord and A Clerk* (1387) if he had known any. See *Lollard Bible*, p. 250.
[4] *Lollard Bible,* p. 1.
[5] *Chronicon Henrici Knighton,* ed. Joseph Rawson Lumby (London, 1889), II, 151-52.
[6] "It is unkyndly for a kniȝt,
That shuld a kynges castel kepe
To bable the Bibel day and niȝt
In resting tyme when he shuld slepe" – *Political Poems and Songs*, ed. T. Wright (RS, 1859), II, 244.
[7] *Lollard Bible,* p. 227.
[8] Henry Hargreaves, "From Bede to Wyclif", *Bulletin John Rylands Library,* 1965, p. 129.
[9] Fristedt argues that Wyclif instigated and oversaw the translation of the early version, and that finding it unsatisfactory, he undertook its revision with his own hand. See the *Wycliffite Bible,* p. 136.
[10] The whole case is presented in David C. Fowler's "John Trevisa and the English Bible", *MP*, LVIII (Nov. 1960), 71-98.
[11] Deanesly, *The Significance of the Lollard Bible* (London, 1951), p. 8.
[12] *Principles and Problems of Biblical Translation* (London, 1955), p. 51.
[13] *Significance,* p. 186.
[14] *Lollard Bible,* p. 203.
[15] *Lollard Bible,* p. 186.
[16] "The Great Bible", ed. Forshall and Madden (Oxford, 1850), which is the source for all quotations from the Bible.
[17] Hargreaves, "From Bede to Wyclif", p. 140.
[18] There are Biblical quotations in the English tracts, but their authenticity is so seriously in doubt that most scholars take the sermons as the safest ground.
[19] W. P. Ker, *Medieval English Literature* (London, 1912), p. 42.
[20] R. W. Chambers, *On the Continuity of English Prose* (*EETS*, OS, 186) (London, 1932), p. xcvi.

5

THE WORDS: DICTION, ALLUSION AND IRONY

It was my contention in Chapter IV that Wyclif's zeal to bring the fourteenth-century Church closer to his idea of New Testament teaching led him to present his case on two distinct levels. The early Wycliffite Bible represents the attempt of scholars to reach a learned audience and reform the Church from the inside, while the later version speaks directly to priests of the lower echelons and to the lay people themselves. In an analogous way, Wyclif's Latin treatises and sermons are organized and worded according to the elaborate *divisios* of the schools, while the English sermons and tracts, stripped of those issues which the Reformer regarded as theological subtleties, argue the same case in terms the people could grasp immediately. In *De Domino Divino,* for example, the debate on the relationship of God's grace to man's merit uses the traditional categories of merit *de condino* and *de congruo,*[1] but in Gospel Sermon XXXIV the same matter is discussed at some length in very simple terms, with only a glancing reference to substance and accident and an insult to Pelagius (an 'ydiot'), betraying the master of the schools (I, 91-92). Wyclif was without doubt the finest theologian at Oxford in his generation, although "his stature was less than Occam's or Bradwardine's" before him,[2] and the strong resistance of the University to the anti-Lollard campaigns of Archbishop Courtenay and his colleagues attests to Wyclif's very strong influence there. Yet with his expulsion from Oxford in 1382 (if Talbert's dating of the sermons is correct, many years earlier[3]), he was able to adopt a new idiom, seek a different audience, and present his whole case on a vastly different level. Perhaps, like his teacher Richard Fitzralph a generation before, he abandoned the debates of the schools with deliberate scorn,[4] seeing there the sterility which later generations frequently found so obvious.

Two things aided Wyclif in shifting from the forms and diction of Oxford to those of his rural parish. The Latin written at Oxford was no longer a pure and effective literary instrument. So cumbersome had it become that one commentator claims the easiest way to understand it is to translate it into English.[5] As a consequence, Wyclif had probably been thinking in English all the time he was writing in Latin. His second advantage was that he used the

Bible a great deal in his scholastic proofs. The language of the parables of Jesus and the figures of Paul and the other epistle-writers kept his mind in touch with common affairs. He was one exception, apparently, to G. R. Owst's implication that the schoolmen had lost touch with 'Life'.[6]

Therefore only rarely does Wyclif have real difficulty in translating a theological concept into idiomatic English, although one can imagine that he often needed to create his own English phrases. Some difficulty is apparent in his attempt to transmit relationships clearly: "And so he was in [the tomb] þree daies, but not bi þes þree daies þere" (II, 52), which apparently means that some part of each of three days Christ remained buried but not all of each day. "Crist seiþ not þat ech in blis is more þan ever is Baptist, but he seiþ þat ech in blis is more þan here is Baptist" (II, 6), means that in heaven each believer is greater than John the Baptist was on the earth. Yet such cases are so rare that the modern reader is startled when he finds obscurity rather than lucidity.

The simplicity of the diction of these sermons is the result of several rather consistently applied techniques. References to his own experiences are excluded. Vocabulary is limited by the employment of common words in new or expanded senses to avoid unfamiliar theological language, and by the explanation or pairing of long or unfamiliar words when they do occur. Bold and colorful language is very common. Insult is often achieved through metaphor, identification of a modern phenomenon with a Biblical one, careful manipulation of the concept of newness, or irony.

There is an extraordinary lack of personal reference of any kind in these sermons. An allusion to the writing of *De Veritate Scripturae:* "In þis mater [the truth of the Bible] we have ynow stryfen in Latyn wiþ adversaries of Goddis lawe . . ." (I, 79) is as close as Wyclif comes to speaking of himself.[7] There are no reminiscenses of childhood places or happenings, no resentment toward named persons, and no allusions to the events of his life. Only ten times in this large corpus does 'I' occur, and then almost exclusively in constructions such as 'I wot' or 'I ween'. This may be interpreted as part of the attempt to make these sermon guides widely useable without change by other Lollard preachers. In addition the impersonality contributes to the effect of simplicity, since almost any mention of Wyclif's mature life would be concerned with scholarly debate and therefore out of the reach of most of his lay audience. The disposition to treat matters of personal concern to him abstractly is another manifestation of a mind that attacks the system which allows abuses rather than the specific abuses themselves.[8]

The vocabulary employed in these sermons is so close to modern usage that Arnold lists fewer than seven hundred words in his gloss to over thirteen hundred fifty pages of Wyclif's sermons and tracts.[9] All but two of these words (*debletis* and *philorgis*) he is able to trace to common Middle English usage. Rolle's *Psalter* was translated with the specific goal of introducing new words from the Vulgate into the vernacular to assist those who knew little or no Latin;[10] Wyclif is just as specifically rejecting that technique in his attempt to "strange not in speche from undirstondinge of þe puple" (I, 79). In order to avoid Latin coinages, Wyclif often expands a native term to express a theological concept. *Unbileveful* (II, 149), is his substitute for incredulous; *undedlynesse* (II, 35), for immortality; *instorid* (II, 253), for contained in; *bie aȝen* for redeem; and *nounpower* (II, 374), or *unpower* (I, 371) for inability. *Byknowe* (II, 243) expresses confess; *even-worþi* (II, 323), equivalent or comparable; *forþinking* (II, 201), repentance; *morynge* (I, 65), making greater; *unholden* (I, 139), under no obligation; *unnobley* (II, 271), ignominy; and *unþank* (I, 256), ill will.

When a long or otherwise difficult term does appear it is very often explained in simpler words or paired with a more familiar term. Wyclif explains extortions as "wrong þat he dide to his neiȝbore" (I, 3), "*an hundred skippis of corn*" (I have followed the printed edition in italicising all quoted scripture), as "more þan a quarter" (I, 22), and "commessaciouns" as "ofte etingis" (II, 224). He employs pairs such as, "God telliþ or specifieþ" (I, 15), and "Crist himsilf expowneþ and seiþ" (I, 27).

Even so, there are some polysyllabic words which look overly Latinate among the homely terms which form their context. *Superfluous* and its derivatives are quite common in the sermons (but never appear in the Bible texts); the OED lists many dates for them a good deal before Wyclif. *Contrariouste* (I, 344; II, 68, 375), appeared in the middle of the fourteenth century and remained in use until at least Lydgate. *Preciousite* (I, 376) is cited first from these sermons, but became widely current in the next century.

Taken with his handling of diction in the sermon texts, which, in my opinion, simplifies and improves on that of the 'Wycliffite' translations, these usages allow the general statement that, when two terms are available, Wyclif usually chooses the more familiar and homely. The phrasing of the sermons is not only unpretentious, it is often colorful or half-figurative as well. Martyrs to a worldly cause are "stynkynge martires" (II, 275), false priests who love neither the bodies nor souls of their people "double traytours" (II, 257), the teaching of modern sects "roten pasturis" (I, 367) for the flocks to graze in, and the teachings of Pelagius "chiding of ydiotis" (I, 91). Any unprofitable speech is likely to be called blabbering and grutching against God. The fiend, if he "have oones man doun, he stireþ him liȝtlier to fouler synnes" (II, 367), and prelates have men "undir foot" (II, 206). If Christ does not confirm the honors bestowed by the pope, they are "not worþ a flye foot" (II, 281), and priests might pray better by observing God's laws "þan to wawe þer lippis" (II, 303). The Christian should be watchful of his affections, "lest þe soule snaperide aftir" (II, 367). The priests of the old law were not offered spacious heaven, but only "a litil holet þat was þe west part of þe tabernacle" (II, 281).

These general characteristics of Wyclif's terminology, together with some special effects, are well exemplified in his handling of insult. Insult is a particularly fertile field for study because there is so much of it in the sermons, based as it is on Wyclif's belief that good preaching includes reproof, even ironic or scornful reproof, following the example of Christ in his words to the woman at the well. It is a kind of writing which gives free play to Wyclif's ungentle imagination and sense of humor. And it is the subject of a good deal of controversy among scholars who wish to describe Wyclif's character. To correct the misconception that all scathing reproof is Wycliffite (a misconception which became popular only after Lollard-hunting became fashionable toward the end of the century), one has to consult literature or orthodox preaching, where the same criticisms were, according to K. B. McFarlane "the veriest commonplaces of fourteenth century controversy".[11]

Wyclif's vituperation customarily follows one of a few distinct patterns. The first involves the use of an image, commonly from the animal world, to pin-point a specific error or failing. (Even in the Latin treatises the new sects are geese, magpies, and mad dogs.[12]) Thus the failure of the sects to warn the people in spiritual matters occurs because the fiend has "stranglid þese houndis wiþ talwe þat þei mai not berke" (I, 247). For strife in the Church like that of "doggis in a poke", Wyclif blames Anticrist, who "haþ put diverse doggis in þe poke of his obedience" (II, 358). Prelates are guilty of pursuing true apostles "as gre-houndis suen an hare" (II, 359). The new rules of the sects are like improperly prepared meat which "makiþ mannis bodi to gurle [growl, gurgle]" (II, 249). Since a full chapter is devoted to metaphor, these examples will be allowed to suggest a larger stock of homely figures. They are representative in that no matter how unsavory the vehicle of the metaphor may be, there is a specific similarity behind the comparison rather than a sweeping condemnation.

A second technique of insult is the identification of the offender with various Biblical personages or prophecies. The third Sunday Gospel sermon establishes the identification of prelates with the Scribes of Jesus' time and monks and friars with the Pharisees (I, 7), a concept which recurs constantly throughout all five groups of sermons. Based on the text in Luke XV, 1, which the preacher translates: "*. . . publicans and sinful men weren comyng to Jesus . . . but scribis and Phariseis gruchiden aȝens þis and blasfemiden aȝens Crist, and seiden, He ete wiþ þem . . .*" (I, 7), Wyclif makes his comparison very specific. Prelates are like Scribes because they murmur against true priests, hope to keep God's commandments entirely in their own hands, and (this embodied in an odd little pun on the word scribe) "writen þe money þat þei pilen of þe peple more bisily þan þei prynten in þer soulis þe knowyng of Goddis lawe".[13] The religious are like Pharisees in their refusal to live as ordinary people, setting themselves apart by "rotun rytys". Both groups in the modern world have the same aims as their New Testament counterparts: to keep true priests from converting sinners by eating with them, to prevent the knowledge that there is freedom in Christ's law, and to keep the people from understanding Christ's general lordship instead of all of "Goddis lawe hongynge on hem for to spule þe puple". Wyclif turns to this set of correspondences time and again in later sermons, sometimes in considerable detail and sometimes with a glancing thrust at "our Pharisees" or "modern Pharisees".

A particularly interesting New Testament identification is that of the Pope and his court with the figure of Antichrist predicted in Relevations. The Spiritual Franciscans of a generation earlier had employed the same piece of abuse and many from that order were Wyclif's close friends during his Oxford career.[14] The Reformer's attitudes reflect the violent historical changes through which the Papacy was passing in Wyclif's lifetime. It is clear from the Latin works that Wyclif objected to the temporal power sought by Gregory XI, not to his claim to be head of the visible Church.[15] Some hope for the purity of the Holy See was felt in the Lollard camp upon the accession of Urban VI, "Our Robert",[16] but enthusiasm for either Pope waned with the development of the Great Schism.[17] Spencer's Crusade, launched by Urban against Clement, solidified Wyclif's opposition to the Papacy itself as an unchristian institution, initiated by the sin of Silvester in accepting the donation of Constantine. After Spencer's Crusade, a reference to Antichrist may be accepted as a reference to the Pope, whoever is holding office. The problem is that these sermons were probably not composed in the order of their appearance in the edition, and perhaps contain some interpolated passages, as Talbert's theory suggests. It would be fruitful to study all the manuscripts in this connection, sorting out the scores of references to Antichrist. For my purposes it is enough to observe that there are at least four different meanings for the term in the sermons, and they are all scattered throughout the five groups.

Sometimes Antichrist means simply the Biblical concept of a spiritual power of hell, as when Wyclif explains that Old Testament prophecy looked forward to the return of Elijah to "fiȝte wiþ Antecrist" (I, 74). At other times the term refers to a specific act or program of Papal power: "As, ȝif þe fend ledde þe pope to kille many þousend men to holde his worldely state, he suede Antecristis maneres" (I, 138). At still others it is directly synonymous with the Papacy, as in this passage: "fulfillinge of mannis lawe is Anticristis riȝtwisness. And so þre degrees ben in þe law of scribis [secular prelates] ; þe first and þe mooste is in þe Popis welle . . ." (I, 15). In addition there are many references for which it is impossible to determine clearly which kind of identification is being made, as when the preacher charges that "Anticrist haþ so weddid þes god is wiþ preestis þat noon may make þis dyvors" (I, 26).

Behind the identification of the Papacy with Antichrist is another, even more frequent charge against the hierarchy. While 'Anticrist' is reserved for the man who holds temporal and spiritual power, any corrupt priest may be called a "lyme of þe fend". The underlying cosmology supposes that "Crist is heed of hooli Chirche, and oþer men ben but his lymes" (II, 36), and a corresponding hierarchy of servants of the devil. "And so is þis world dyvydid in two maner of lordshipis þat ben Goddis and þe fendis, for al$_3$if þe fend have no propre lordship, neþeles he calengiþ to have greet lordshipe" (I, 36). Wyclif took Augustine's metaphoric description of the two cities, Jerusalem and Babylon, very literally. Each city was, for him, "constituted eternally, and the destiny of every member irrevocable".[18] The effect of this way of seeing the world and especially the Church influences Wyclif's diction on every page. The presence of the 'fend' and his 'lymes' is as real, and demands mention as casual, as the presence of anything else in the world. Yet there is no attempt to visualize devils, as in scores of differently-oriented medieval sermons and devotional tracts, or give them a personal reference in the preacher's experience, as in the colorful accounts by Martin Luther of his dreams. To Wyclif the devil remains a spiritual power, manifesting itself in its perversion of God's purposes, and it is the manifestation which is depicted with descriptive power.

A third manner of insult Wyclif frequently offers is the charge of newness. The underlying assumption is, of course, that the New Testament Church was as close to perfection as it is possible for a human institution to be, and any departure from its practices must be considered degeneration. The constant charge against the monks and friars, then, is that they have added to "Cristis religioun", and "noon addicioun is worþ but $_3$if Goddis lawe grounde it" (I, 40). This assumption follows directly from Wyclif's reliance on the sufficiency of the Bible and his placing the traditions of the Church in a much less important role. Christian life, therefore, was complete and perfect only at first; it is the same to call a thing an innovation as to ask for its rejection. The newness of the "new sects" is itself a charge against them, and an opposition is created between the "newe sects" and "Crist's sect" (I, 20).

A fourth method of insult is irony. Canon Shirley noted it as one of the distinguishing marks of Wyclif's style, attributing to it keenness and delicacy.[19] If those epithets are taken to mean that the object of the irony is specific and the words chosen for their economy and cutting edge, one must immediately accept them. There is, in addition, an off-handed quality about the ironic comment which strengthens it and makes it seem that the reader or listener had thought of it himself. For example, Wyclif says that unlawful love of worldly possessions "falliþ in religiouse and in oþir men of þe worlde" (II, 295). Classing the religious (by which, of course, he means men and women in orders) as men of the world is an ironic reversal of the meaning of that title, and the off-hand manner of its presentation is the tacit assumption that it will be granted. The effectiveness of very much of the irony which has impressed Wyclif's critics over the years lies in this lightness of touch.

The Pope and his court are frequently the subjects of this ironic tendency. The Pope's letters of indulgence, Wyclif comments, will not defend a man against God (I, 68); and later they are said to "do good for to covere mostard pottis, but not þus for to wynne men blis . . ." (I, 381). Of Popes' wars, "Joon tauȝte never þis charite . . ." (II, 319). Of Papal dispensation, ". . . and ask hem not leve of þe pope to fle from yvel to Cristis lawe" (II, 319). And of Papal appointments, "But popis chesyn, for moneie or for preier of princis, many men þat ben unable to bere haly water in chirchis" (I, 304).

The sects come in for their share of ironic comment: "For he puttiþ to Jesus Crist boþe cursing and disseit, whan he seiþ bi his dede þat Crist hidde þe beter wey, and tauȝt þe unperfit wey, til þat God had sent þes sectis" (II, 337-8). This claimed superiority of the religious is a constant target for Wyclif's attacks. The policy of cloistering is another: "And here is risun a newe ordre, to close men quyk in stoones . . . but ȝif a man were wood, it myȝte do good to close him þus" (II, 52). A third is the relation to money, for some apparently had claimed that religious men should be rich because money is a good, which is like saying of "þeves, þat þei ben more hardi men, whi shulden þei not have þe goodis þat þei robben fro oþer men?" (I, 315). More succinct and cutting are these gibes: "ȝif Crist hadde do þis myracle for hyre, þanne þes Fariseis hadden wel argued" (II, 198), and "Poul doiþ not þis for moneie, ne to gete him annuel rente, but for pure charite" (II, 369).

The irony, then, like other methods of insult, always has a specific point to make. It may be argued that the abuses Wyclif castigates are exaggerated (although the chroniclers and orthodox preachers observe much the same thing) but not that he expresses his contempt in indiscriminate language.

There can be no doubt that Wyclif's doctrinal statements benefit from their translation into the homely and practical terms of weekly preaching to a lay flock. The requirements of his audience demanded that the preacher strip his presentation of the verbal quibbles and deliberate subtleties with which the Latin sermons and treatises are blemished. What remains carries the weight of a viewpoint firmly conceived and expressed: "And herfore worche we wiseli, and fiȝte we aȝens þe fend, siþ þis stondiþ wiþ Goddis lawe and wiþ fillinge of Goddis wille" (I, 98), and "Stonde a man in vertu and treuþe, and al þis world overcomeþ not him" (I, 370).

1 *Latin Works*, X, ed. R. L. Poole (Wyclif Society; London, 1890), Bk iii.

2 *Chronicon Henrici Knighton,* ed. Joseph Rawson Lumby (London, 1889), II, 151 and May McKisack, *The Fourteenth Century, 1307-1399* (Oxford, 1959), p. 514.

3 E. W. Talbert, "The Date of the Composition of the English Wycliffite Collection of Sermons", *Speculum,* XII (October, 1937), 464-74.

4 Reginald Lane Poole, "Richard Fitzralph", *Dictionary of National Biography,* XIX, 194.

[5] Reginald Lane Poole, *Wycliffe and Movements for Reform* (London, 1889), p. 85. In his introduction to *Latin Works*, II, Poole explains his five reasons for thinking so, XXI.
[6] *Literature and the Pulpit* (Cambridge, England, 1933), p. 55.
[7] The lack of personal reference is, of course, one of the difficulties involved in dating these sermons and determining their authorship conclusively. Even this reference might describe a lost Latin work, either by Wyclif or one of his group, although it describes *De Veritate* better than any other surviving tract.
[8] This is a chief difference between Wyclif and other fourteenth-century critics of the Church. Wyclif attacked foundations where others whose orthodoxy was never questioned had equally scathing things to say about the individual prelates or friars. See David Knowles, *Saints and Scholars* (Cambridge, England, 1962), pp. 144-45.
[9] The gloss appears at the end of volume III of *Select English Works* where the sermons and tracts are treated together. Considered separately, the gloss for the sermons would undoubtedly include far fewer than seven hundred items.
[10] *English Writings of Richard Rolle*, ed. Hope Emily Allen (London, 1931), p. 8.
[11] *John Wycliffe and the Beginnings of English Nonconformity* (London, 1952), pp. 95-96.
[12] *De Apostasia, Latin Works* IX, ed. M. H. Dziewicki (Wyclif Society; London, 1889), 28, 42, and 82.
[13] Punning was common even within the solemn circle of formal preaching. See G. R. Owst's *Literature and the Pulpit* (Cambridge, England, 1933), p. 84 and *Preaching in Medieval England* (Cambridge, England, 1926), p. 329.
[14] Four doctors from the mendicant orders appeared in Wyclif's behalf during his trial at St. Paul's in 1377.
[15] *De Domino Divino*, Ch. 11.
[16] *De Potestate Pape, Latin Works*, III, ed. J. Loserth (Wyclif Society; London, 1907), 233.
[17] *De Potestate Pape*, 247.
[18] Gordon Leff, *Heresy in the Later Middle Ages* (Manchester, 1967), II, 518.
[19] *Fasciculi Zizaniorum*, ed. W. W. Shirley (London, 1858), p. XXI.

6

THE STRUCTURES: THE SERMON AND THE SENTENCE

The choice of a terminology for his precepts was an important one for Wyclif, but it was only one aspect of the adjustment he had to make when he decided to take his case before the people in the English idiom. A second part of his problem was, of course, how to form intelligible and effective structures with the terms he had chosen.

One way of considering literary prose, a very instructive one I think, is proposed by Northrop Frye: "Actual prose is the expression or imitation of directed thinking or controlled description in words, and its unit is the sentence. It does not follow that all prose is descriptive or thoughtful, much less logical, but only that prose imitates, in its rhythm and structure, the verbal expression of a conscious and rational mind".[1] Frye distinguishes such prose from the language of drama and fiction which conforms to the rhythm of association rather than discourse, as well as from the various rhythms of poetry. Structure may be considered in the relationships between units (i.e. sentences, in Frye's analysis) and in the relationships within units; in Wyclif's prose there is a ready analogy between these levels of organization. This suggests that Frye's thesis might be extended to posit that a particular method of structuring is habitual or attractive to a particular kind of rational mind. The content of Wyclif's sermons and treatises, both in Latin and in English, reveals a constant preoccupation with the differences he saw between New Testament teaching and fourteenth-century Christianity. The principles of organization in the English sermons are consequently those of comparison and contrast, in the English sentences, those of parallelism, balance, and antithesis. It is hoped that the approach to Wyclif's prose through what appears to be his own method may reveal more of its excellence than have earlier, more impressionistic, comments.

The traditional estimate of Wyclif's effectiveness in prose expression is high. G. P. Krapp reasserts the claim of the Reformer as "father of English prose", on the grounds that he was the first Englishman to grasp "the broad principles which underlie prose expression", and "the first intelligent writer of English prose".[2] If literary prose is given the interpretation of Northrop Frye's remark, such a judgement of Wyclif's work is no longer possible.

Certainly there are prose pieces throughout the earlier history of the language which imitate "the verbal expressions of a conscious and rational mind".[3] Still more tenuous is the attribution of unity to the sermons in an attempt to confirm their excellence. Krapp calls each sermon "a compact and unified discussion of a single theme".[4] One of the very sermons he uses to illustrate his contention compares hunters with fishermen, charges that gentlemen hunt on Sunday, discusses what will be eaten in Paradise, points out the homicidal tendencies of friars, refers to the invention of gunpowder, and alleges that foreign friars are plotting to kill Englishmen. Such a progression does not invite praise for compactness and unity of the usual kind; if the sermon is to be evaluated, its organization must be sought in something other than thematic unity. The principle of contrast explains what simple unity does not, for each of the subjects mentioned in the sermon is chosen for its specific violation of some facet of the text which Wyclif is explaining.

Krapp also thinks of the sentences as unified: "The many-membered, sprawling sentence, found in most early writers of English prose is not characteristic of Wyclif".[5] Yet the first three sermons contain several sentences of over ninety words and none of less than thirteen. Again the principle of contrast explains what simple unity does not, for even the longest sentences are frequently saved from unintelligibility by their careful balance of clauses and phrases. There are grounds for agreeing with a high estimate of Wyclif's prose, but they are not those which Krapp adduces–priority in his use of the prose structure and unity of the sermon and the sentence. I shall try to describe Wyclif's structures and some of their relationships to other fourteenth-century prose, emphasizing the feature which seems to me consistent and distinctive, i.e., their use of contrast.

These sermons do not begin with either of the two standard gambits of learned preaching. There is no prayer that God will move the hearts of the people and no opening authority, *exemplum,* or argument from natural reason.[6] It is rare to find even a reference to the day on which the sermon text is to be read, although the texts are those designated for the days of the liturgical year. There is no address to the audience. The text is stated with a sparse introductory phrase like, "Crist telliþ in þis parable . . ." (I, 1), or "Þis gospel biddiþ Cristene men . . ." (I, 19). The Scriptural text is either presented fully at the beginning of the sermon, as is usual with narrative material (I, nos. V and VII), or sentence by sentence throughout the sermon, as with expository passages (I, nos. I-IV). Textual commentary is of two kinds, historical clarifications like the explanation of 'Abrahames bosom' (I, 2), 'raby' (I, 158), Pentecost (II, 305), and New Testament units of measure (I, 9, 22), and allegorical interpretations, which are explained just after the quotations of the text. These comments appear very frequently, although not in absolutely every sermon. There is only one feature of the Scriptural exegesis which is never absent: the contrast of the New Testament teaching with religious life in Wyclif's own time. This is the form which holds each sermon in a kind of loose unity, even when the text for the day suggests more than one theme, or an incomplete theme. There is no attempt to dramatize the message by giving it an *exemplum* or even a proverbial statement at the end of the sermon. Either the sermon ends abruptly when the last phrase of the text is explained or it summarizes briefly the lesson to be learned in a construction like, "And so we . . ." and "And herfore . . .".

Two sample sermons will make the technique clearer. Number XI in the Sunday Gospel series (I, 27-29), is typical of those sermons in which the text is translated as a unit at the beginning of the sermon. In this case the passage is the parable of Jesus concerning the Pharisee and the publican. Following the translation the preacher clarifies the main point at issue–the warning against hypocrisy, which is "þe first spice of pride". The next remarks ostensibly describe the New Testament Pharisees, but at the same time indicate a danger to the church of any era in maintaining a group professionally religious. Clearly Wyclif is talking about the church of his own day when he mentions the "sectis newe", and even more specifically the "monkes, chanouns, and freris" a few sentences later. Once these groups have been identified with the Pharisees of Jesus' day, their faults may be discussed as if the words of the Bible had referred directly to them. The rest of the sermon simply exploits that method; each statement of Christ and each implication from his words is followed by a corresponding charge against the sects.

The other main method, sentence-by-sentence explanation of the text, is exemplified in Number XXXII of the Sunday Epistles (II, 317-322). The sermon begins with a one-paragraph introduction to the text, explaining the difference between worldly and Christian men. In paragraph two, the first and second sentences of the text (on the translation of believers from death to life), are presented and explained briefly, and the contrast with contemporary life introduced in these words: "And þis translacioun is better þan worldly translacioun of þe pope . . .". Paragraph three contains three more Biblical sentences, their explanations, and this contrast: "And þis shulden Cristen men loke, what law sownned to charite . . . . And herfore ben sum men moved to leve þes four newe sectis . . . ." In paragraph four the Biblical quotation urges the sacrifice of life for one's brother and arouses the preacher's anger thus: "Lord, where þis pope Urbane hadde Goddis charite dwelling in him, whan he stirede men to fiȝte and slee many þousaund men, to venge him on þe toþer pope, and of men þat holden wiþ him! ȝif þat Goddis lawe be trewe, þis was an opyn fendis turn". The next sentence of the text, translated in paragraph five, enjoins generosity, which the preacher contrasts with the alms-begging of "tirauntis and strong beggers". Paragraph six, on brotherhood, contrasts the kinship of true Christians with the begging friars who are "not oure breþeren, but Phariseis". The final paragraph is a comment on the test for sincerity which consists in doing good work and speaking truth, rather than pretending to be hungry to get money. The last two sentences seem to be a sort of plea to the strong beggars to follow the commands of the Bible.

Whichever format is used for the presentation of the texts, the principle of contrast is apparent in the sermon. A similar structural principle may be seen in a large number of the sentences. The reader who looks for "short, nervous sentences",[7] "short, well-constructed, usually unified"[8] sentences, or "terse, homely English",[9] may be seriously disillusioned by an average sentence length of 42.9 words in the first three sermons of Arnold's edition. Admittedly, the sentence divisions are made at the discretion of the editor, and may be interpreted differently by other readers of the manuscript. Arnold himself, I believe, changed his method of sentence division as his work progressed. This I infer from the very great difference in sentence length between the first three sermons of the Sunday Gospel set (printed first by Arnold), and the first three sermons of each of the other four sets. Statistical analysis shows the difference to be "highly significant".[10] The other stylistic features observed remain highly consistent from one group of sermons to another; especially close are the Sunday Gospels and the Sunday Epistles, and good manuscript evidence has been found for believing them to have been composed for the same liturgical year.[11] There is nothing in the sermons themselves to suggest that Wyclif was, for any reason, deliberately producing shorter sentences in the later groups of sermons. A more reasonable theory is that the editor found that the sentences might be marked off in several ways, and that for greater intelligibility he increasingly marked off shorter ones. One test for such a theory is to count the number of coordinating conjunctions which appear as the first words in the edited sentences. If Arnold is responsible for the shortness of the sentences of later sermons, it should be reflected in a greater percentage of conjunctions at the beginning of the sentences of later sermons.[12] This is exactly the case; only 41.8 percent of the sentences of the Sunday Gospel sermons begin with coordinating conjunctions, while 73.7 percent of those of the Sunday Epistle sermons do so. (See Appendix A.) The manuscript indicates unambiguous junctures only at what Arnold has marked as paragraph divisions, and Henry Hargreaves met this problem by treating each independent clause as a sentence in his analysis of sentence length.[13]

Variation in sentence length from one set of sermons to another is not, then, a feature of Wyclif's style, but of Arnold's edition. Variation within each sermon, on the other hand, is Wyclif's. Even when a separate sentence is marked for almost every independent element, as it is in Arnold's division of the Sunday Epistle sermon sentences, the range of sentence lengths extends from seven words to ninety-three. The 29.0 word average sentence length of the sentences in the four later sermon groups (see Appendix B), does not, in any case, indicate brevity or terseness, as the traditional view of Wyclif's style asserts.

The fact that such a large number of the sentences begin with coordinating conjunctions, or, from the point of view of the manuscript, that there are so few unambiguous breaks in the narrative, is itself relevant to Wyclif's style. The heavy use of coordinating conjunctions produces an effect of continuity and logical flow, especially within paragraphs, which sometimes suggests a closer relationship between ideas than actually exists, or at any rate, than modern observers would postulate. An intriguing example is found in a sermon on the Canaanite woman who sought Jesus' blessing for her daughter: "... heþene folk dwelten þere [in Canaan] til þat Crist came. And so þis paynym womman is þe substans of mennis soule ... And suche a soule wendiþ out of þe coostis of Chanaan, ffor it forsakiþ þe paynym life þat it was before inne" (I, 115). The reader or listener is led by such a technique very quickly from an historical observation to its 'anagogik' interpretation.

In order to describe the complexity of sentence structures, I have adapted a technique devised by Maynard Merlyn Eyestone for describing subordinate clause 'nesting' in American English.[14] His practice is to make an elliptical diagram of the subordinate clauses, showing their relationship in both depth and width. A sentence with four subordinate clauses may be a relatively straightforward expression, as is this example from the Sunday Epistle sermons: "For as angelis weren not confermed, but ever stoden in ny$_3$t of grace, so mankynde, siþ it was made, stood sum wey in ny$_3$t of synne, til þat Crist was maad man; and he is sunne of ri$_3$twisnesse, and he mai not falle to synne, siþ he is ri$_3$twisnes him silf" (II, 222-23). An elliptical diagram of that sentence would show only one level of subordination, no clause nests ⬭ S ⬭ V ⬭ + SV Compl + SV ⬭. A sentence from the Sunday Gospels of approximately the same length has a nest of four-clause depth, which is as deep as any written sentence in Eyestone's study.[15] "Þe stori telleþ;–*Þere was a riche man* þat disuside his richesse in pride and in glotonye, for he was *cloþid in purpur and bise,* þat ben prescious cloþes boþe rede and white; and so he was an ypocrite, þat shewide him to þe world boþe austerne and clene, as worldly men done" (I, 1), would give this diagram:

Eyestone's method thus provides a convenient measure for the complexity of clause relationships. Such complexity does not correlate directly with difficulty or obscurity of style. As the examples from *The Cloud of Unknowing* and Chaucer's "Prologue" to the *Astrolabe* show, a careful organization of thought renders even four-clause nests immediately clear. On the other hand, it is in wide, and/or deep, nests that difficulty in understanding is most likely to occur. A highly nested style, then, may be either lucid or opaque, but a style free of subordination will be recognized by most readers as structurally simple. Furthermore, there is an undeniable relationship between the complexity of the ideas with which a writer is dealing, in these cases at least, and the verbal structures in which he expresses them. The writers of *Mandeville's Travels, The Festial,* and *Speculum Christiani* are popularizers. Trevisa, Chaucer and Usk expect a more learned and sophisticated audience; while the mystics have in mind their own disciples or potential disciples, from whom they may expect more than usual spiritual refinement. The preacher who addresses his colleagues at Oxford expects his subtilties and qualifications to be understood; the rural curate would be pretentious if he adopted them.

The Eyestone technique gives objective testimony to the impressions most readers have of the complexity of these samples of prose. *Mandeville's Travels* exhibits very little subordination, containing only four clause nets in Chapter I and none of a depth of more than two. *Speculum Christiani* includes a whole sermon in which there is only one nest of a depth of two. The first sermon in Mirk's *Festial* only contains four clause nests, all two clauses deep; a later sermon has a sentence with a four-clause nest, although the rest of that sermon only has four other nests two clauses deep.

Half of the sentences in Richard Rolle's "The Bee and the Stork" contain nests, two are three deep, and four are two or more wide. Since Rolle's sentences also usually contain several independent elements, a structure like this one sometimes results: SV Compl + SV + SV + SV + SV Compl

The author of the *Cloud of Unknowing* is capable of a great deal of sophistication in the handling of sentence patterns. In Chapter I, for example, more than half his sentences contain clause nests, the more complex sentences being followed by short questions like: "And what more?" and "Bot what did he?". This author is able to make his point perfectly clear through a sequence of clauses arranged thus:

Chaucer's "Prologue" to the *Treatise on the Astrolabe* exhibits a moderate amount of nesting; in the distribution of subordinate clauses and the configurations of clause nests, the "Prologue" closely resembles Thomas Usk's "Prologue" to *The Testament of Love,* which was in the past attributed to

Chaucer. Trevisa rarely produces a sentence with a nest deeper than two, but one utterance of Miles in the *Dialogus* presents this pattern:

An 'old' type sermon in *Middle English Sermons* exhibits only three clause nests in its sentences, although one does reach a depth of three. The 'modern' or 'university' sermon, however, is made up of distinctively complex sentences whose clause nests are both wide and deep. This sentence is so complex as to be difficult to untangle:

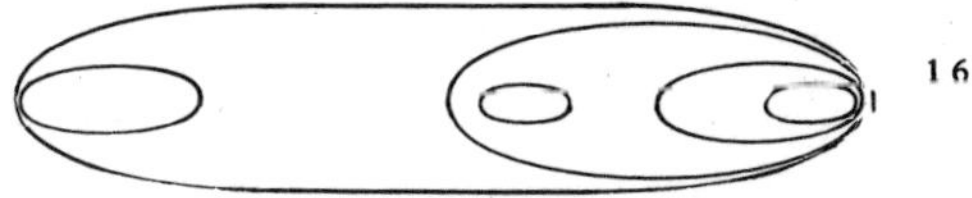 [16]

This preacher himself seems to forget his place in the clause sequence when he says "... as Moyses was, þe wiche, as þe Maister of þe Stories seyþ in ys second boke vppon scripture, seyþ þat he was a gret philosofre ...". Anacoluthon is rather common with this writer, especially in clauses which report or acknowledge quotations. He is the only writer in my sample with a characteristically difficult style.

A selection of Wyclif's sentences are diagrammed in Appendix C. They are, in general, more complex than Chaucer's and less complex than those of the university sermon. Of the one hundred twenty three sentences, eighty-seven percent exhibit some subordination and of those, thirty-nine percent contain clause nests. Two of the nests are four clauses deep. The first, an early sentence in the Sunday Gospel series, has already been reported. It presents no difficulty for the reader and no signs of anacoluthon in its formation, in spite of its complex structure. The organization of the other sentence is unclear. In the middle of Sermon I of the Sunday Epistle group is found: "To þis entent spekiþ Poul, in þe persone of al holy Chirche, ^{a}(þat now, ^{b}(whanne tyme is passid to bileve ^{c}(þat þe Incarnacioun is to come,)^{c} but ^{d}(þat þe Incarnacioun is passid,)^{d} ^{e}(as þe Chirche seeþ ascencioun,)^{e} it mut nedis now be nere to þe ful helþe of þe Chirche ^{f}(þan it was bifore tyme ^{g}(whanne þe Chirche oonly bilevede")^{f})^{g})^{a} (II, 222). The difficulty concerns clause *d*. Either it is coordinate with *b* and the *but* disrupts the clarity of the relationship; or it is coordinate with *c* (i.e. the second object of 'bileve'), and the sense is lost. This confusion of clause roles is the only case of its kind among these one hundred twenty three sentences. Similar structural difficulties are present, although not frequently, throughout the corpus.

The subordinate clauses may occur in either substantive or modifying roles within the sentences. They are very commonly the objects of verbs which indicate quotation, either direct or indirect. They are also used as subjects and auxiliaries to the expletive *it.* They may modify nouns, verbs, other modifiers, or, as is very common, the whole sentence.

Often participial constructions replace subordinate clauses, usually as modifiers for substantives. Sometimes these constructions sound abrupt and unidiomatic, as if they had been translated from Latin with too little care for the rhythm of the English version. For example, "*Abraham seide to þe riche man*, dampnyd, *Sone* . . ." (I, 2), and "þis servant sent out is the manheed of Crist" (I, 4), are not easy English. However, other similar constructions seem completely natural: "*a vois cam of þe cloude, seiyng, Þis is my loved sone* . . ." (II, 58), and "*þei weren baptised in Jordan shryvyng to God þer synnes*" (II, 5). Sometimes such a treatment gives the sentence an unexpected conciseness and polish, as "For Anticristis lawe, cloutid of many, is full of errors" (I, 4), and "ech man shal do good, supposinge þat he dwelliþ in God" (I, 167).

The appendix of sentence diagrams also shows the arrangements of the sentence elements. By far the most frequent pattern is SV Obj. When the order, as in Wyclif's: "how suen þei Baptist, þat þus evermore reversen usage. Fernand Mossé describes five occasions for variation of the SV Obj. order.[17] The question transformation in Middle English usually required VS Obj. order, as in Wyclif's "how suen þei Baptist, þat þus evermore reversen him?" (II, 3). Imperative constructions form a second class of irregularities: "*heere þei hem* spedely, and kepe þei Goddis commandementis" (I, 3), "But leve we þis" (I, 171), "Drede we not" (II, 4), and "*Do ȝe penaunce*" (II, 4). A third occasion for abnormal sentence order occurs in sentences which begin with adverbial adjuncts: "to sichc bodili pore men techeþ þis gospel men to do her almes" (1, 6), "And bi þis was shewide the frendship" (I, 171); with adverbs of time: "*Now shal Y not clepe ȝou servauntis*" (I, 170), "*þanne went out to Joon þe peple of Jerusalem*" (II, 5); adverbs of place, "Here may we see" (I, 2); and adverbs of connection, "herfore traveilide Poul" (I, 169), "so eet Baptist eerbis and hony" (II, 5). There are cases of Obj. VS order when the object requires particular emphasis: "þis ryver of Galile likide Crist ofte to wende biside it" (I, 301), "oþer housis hadde he noon" (II, 3), and "þat mut God himsilf do" (II, 4). The only examples of inversion not mentioned by Mossé among these common types consist of acknowledgement of speaker in expressions like "seiþ Crist" (I, 166, 170), and "rehersiþ Crist" (I, 167), which writers of Modern English use for the same purpose in prose narrative and fiction.

A single adjective is found before the noun without exception in this sample. Two adjectives usually appear after the substantive, linked by 'and' and often preceded by 'both', as "cloþes boþe rede and white" (I, 1), "*a myche void place stablid betwene hem, derke and unordynel*" (I, 2), "þer enemyes, boþe religiouse and oþer" (II, 226). Predicate adjectives also frequently appear with 'both . . . and', as in, "þat shewide him to þe world boþe austerne and clene" (I, 1), and in pairs without 'both', "þe peeple is grete and many" (I, 4), and "as comune þing is betere and bifore oþer þingis" (I, 165). Less typical of Wyclif is the placement of one adjective before and one after the noun, but there are a few cases: "þe last good and best" (I, 4).

The article, when it appears, always precedes the noun or attributive adjective. Wyclif often, however, omits the article where modern usage supplies it, producing an unidiomatic abruptness which is for modern ears the strangest thing in his style. There are countless examples throughout the sermons: "bi treuþe þat God tolde him" (I, 2), "by dampnyng of hise breþren" (I, 3), "by synne of man tyme is lost" (II, 221), "sunne of ri$_3$twisnesse is uppe" (II, 222). Other Middle English writers who were familiar with Latin exhibit this same trait. Chaucer's translation *Boece* contains many examples: "But tyme is now", "comyn to corage of a parfit man", "God is bygynnynge of al", and "But now is tyme that thou drynke . . .".[18] His prologue to the *Astrolabe*, however, will not yield a single case.[19] Wyclif's practice is to display this stylistic mannerism in both translation and original composition.

Adverbs and adverbial phrases are usually found after the verb, sometimes after the object, but more frequently before it. The most common arrangement, therefore, is V Adv. Obj., as in "þei swagen in a maner þe peyne" (I, 2), "þat doiþ specialy his greet almes" (I, 6), "God $_3$yve freely tyme" (II, 221), and "bryngen in li$_3$tli þes two" (II, 224). One also finds V Obj. Adv., as "he sufferide peyne paciently and þow toke þi lusts synfulli" (1, 2), and Adv. V, as "li$_3$tli wole a riche man" (1, 1), and "men li$_3$tli acorden" (I, 170). Another frequently-occurring pattern is the interruption of the verb phrase by an adverb: "*he is now confortid and þou art now turmentid*" (I, 2), "þis shall ever last" (I, 4). Wyclif's choice of subordinating conjunctions is shown by Henry Hargreaves in "Wyclif's Prose" to conform to the "general development of the language since his time".[20]

The devices Wyclif uses for negation are similar to those of Modern English, except in three cases. One is the use of 'not' after a simple verb, where modern usage demands that it be placed between the parts of a verb phrase: "filleþ not hevene" (I, 6), "done not þer office" (I, 166), "who þat dwelliþ not in him" (I, 167), and "bodili si$_3$t cam not þanne" (I, 298). A second is the agglutination of the negative with 'is' and 'will be', as "þere nys no man" (I, 4). Double negatives, very common in Middle English, form a third class of unmodern usages: "ne witen not where it be" (I, 168).

Sequence of tenses is carefully observed in these sermons. Sometimes this poses no small difficulty, as when the text contains a prophecy which the preacher reports as fulfilled:

> "And so tellip our bileve in storye of þe gospel, *þat Jesus seynge Jerusalem wepte þeron . . . and seide þat if þou knewe* þus synne, þou shuldist wepe as Y do nowe . . . *for alle þes þingis*, þat þou shuldist cunne *ben now hidde fro þi iȝen. For daies shal come in þee . . . and þin enemyes schulen envyron þee as a palis al aboute . . . and þei shal not leve in þee stoon liynge upon a stoon* . . . Alle þes wordis weren shewide in dede" (I, 24-25).

A strict observance of sequence of tenses, involving a present, present participle, preterit, conditional, future, and passive preterit, shows some care by the author for the clarity of his language. In some translations, however, sequence of tenses is sacrificed to the import of the words of the Vulgate. For example, Wyclif translates "*Factum est autem ut moreretur mendicus*", as "*it is maad* by Goddis wille *þat þis begger was deed*" (I, 1), "*Et misit servum suum hora coene dicere invitatis ut venirent, quia jam parata sunt omnia*", as "*he sente out his servauntis in houre of þis soper to seie to men clepid hereto to come, for now alle þingis ben rede*" (I, 4), and "*antequam Abraham fieret, ego sum*" as "Biforn þat Abraham shulde be, Y am" (I, 127). All three translations, and others like them, do not look like careless violations of English language habits as much as attempts to preserve the eternal implications of the Latin *est, sunt,* and *sum*. "It was made" (by God's will), is not the same thing as "it is made"; the loss is the sense of continuing action, or perhaps of action outside of measured time.[21] The reasoning applies to "all þingis ben redy"—they were, are and will be—and to Jesus' affirmation "Y am".

The sentences are not all beautifully constructed, nor are they all free of obscurity or redundancy, but few, if any, will fail, for syntactic reasons, to be understood by a modern reader. On the whole they offer a sophisticated theology in lucid, readable English. The structural devices which most often contribute to the orderliness of Wyclif's sentences are parallelism, balance, and antithesis. These devices are used, not lyrically, as with the mystics, but logically, as a smaller-scale embodiment of the principle of comparison and contrast which orders the sermon method. Obvious forms like 'as . . . so' and 'neither . . . nor' are the organizing elements in many of his sentences or parts of his sentences, for example "as seintis in hevene wanten envye, so dampned men failen in charite" (I, 3), "as þer is þre maner of synne, so þre maner men excusiden hem" (I, 5), and "men may neiþer falle fro hevene to helle, ne flee fro helle to hevene" (I, 2). In "As men shulden trowe in Crist þat he is boþe God and man, so men shulden trowe bi hise wordis þat þei ben soþe" (II, 1), an additional effect of balance is produced by the use of a dependent 'þat' clause in each half of the sentence. The balanced rhythm is reinforced by the repetition of 'offrid' in this case: "For as þe Pask lombe was offrid of oo ȝeer wiþouten wemm, so Crist was offrid at Pask to bie his Chirche . . ." (I, 296).

Wyclif also effects rhythmic balance without the commonly used conjunctions. For example, "he sufferide peyne paciently and þow toke þi lusts synfulli" (I, 2), "and lordis for þer profit moten nedes helpe herto, and Anticristis feynynge mote nedes be knowun" (I, 6), and "þe mercy of God is more þan is envie of þe fend, and goodness of God is more þan is hate of þe fend" (I, 278).

Often the phrases are held in a more complex relationship, some in balance, and some in antithesis, as "So shulden preestis in þis worlde shapen her lyf to Cristis Chirche, not to be enheritid here, ne to be riche, ne to fiȝte, but to teche Cristis lore boþe in her lyf and in her word" (I, 167). "And so þat þing þat þou trowist here, þou seest not here wiþ þi iȝen, but þow trowist it above hope, and bilevest it bineþ science" (I, 168), almost reminds one of Dame Julian's handling of rhythm.

Sometimes the balance produces irony: the ascension should teach the "breþeren goostly werkes of mercy, not oonly wiþ comounnes but also wiþ prelatis" (I, 132), friars should "leve her heye housis þat þei propren unto hem, siþ Crist hadde no propre hous to reste in his heed" (I, 58), "Poul doiþ not þis for moneie, ne to gete him annuel rente, but for pure charite" (II, 369), and "And herwiþ þei seien to men þat þei passen bishopis and popis, and certis þei seien here þe soþe, if þei menen passinge in synne" (I, 178).

In his rare lyrical moods, Wyclif shows himself capable of moving rhetorical effect, much of it produced through a balance of clauses. He explains why the lord of the feast, when he was refused by his first invited guests, asked for "pore feble men, pore blynde men, and pore lame men" to be brought instead:

> "And it semeth þat þese and noon oþer shal come to hevene, for who shal come to hevene but if he be pore in spirit; who shal come to heven but ȝif he be feble in spirit and nedid to have mercy; who shall come to hevene but ȝif he bi liȝtned of his blindnesse; and who shal come to hevene, but he þat halteþ now hiȝe in vertues and now low in synnes?" (I, 5)

In a passage on the text *"If þe world hate you"*, Wyclif writes a series of balanced sentences:

> "If þou grutche aȝens proverte, and coveite worldeli worshipe, wite þou þat Crist bifore was porer þan þou, siþ he hadde not bi his manhede place to reste his heed ynne. If þou grutchist þat þi sugetis wolen not ȝyve þee goodis, þenke how Cristis sugettis wolden neiþer ȝyve him mete ne

> herberwe; and ȝit herfore he curside hem not, but dide hem moche good. And if þou grutche þat þe world doiþ þee ony injurie, and þou profitist to þe world aȝen in love and mekenesse; þenke how Crist bifore þee profitide þus more to þe worlde; and ȝit Crist suffride more wronge of hise sugettis þan þou maist" (I, 172-3)

Often the balanced structures embody a figurative and a literal counterpart. To clarify the mission of John the Baptist, Wyclif says "As a vois is a soun þe which is formed of a mouþ . . . so Joon Baptist was foormed of the word of Goddis mouþ", and "But as a vois bereþ þe witt of þe word wiþinne þe soule, so Baptist bare þe witt of Goddis word wiþouten error" (II, 4). To explain Jesus' reference to fruit trees he says, "as þes trees han not of kynde to brynge to men siche fruytis; so siche children of þe fend feden not men goostly" (I, 21). Many of the images discussed in Chapter VII are formed in a similar way.

Wyclif's prose does not exhibit the lyric tenderness and sensitivity of *Revelations of Divine Love* or *The Cloud of Unknowing,* nor does it imitate a flow of consciousness as does *Mandeville's Travels* with its display of what may be studied ingenuousness. It is, structurally at least, literal-minded and unrelievedly straightforward. Yet it does rather surprisingly fulfill its own desideratum: to "strange not in speche from understonding of the peple".

[1] *The Well-Tempered Critic* (Princeton, 1955), p. 18.

[2] *The Rise of English Literary Prose* (Oxford, New York, 1915), p. ix.

[3] For a thorough discussion of Wyclif's predecessors in prose expression, see R. W. Chambers, *On the Continuity of English Prose* (EETS, OS, 187) (London, 1932).

[4] *English Literary Prose,* p. 48.

[5] *English Literary Prose,* p. 50.

[6] A summary of the various theories of sermon composition current in the fourteenth century is given by Woodburn O. Ross in his introduction to *Middle English Sermons* (*EETS,* OS, 209) (London, 1940). Sermon openings are discussed on p. xxi.

[7] W. W. Shirley, "Introduction", *Fasciculi Zizaniorum* (London, 1858), p. xxi.

[8] *English Literary Prose,* p. 50.

[9] Herbert Brook Workman, *The Dawn of the Reformation* (London, 1933), p. 193.

[10] The number of words per sentence in the first three sermons of group I were compared with that of the first three sermons of each of the other groups by using the TF test of statistical significance; see Bernard Ostle, *Statistics in Research* (Ames, Iowa, 1956), pp. 45-49. 'Highly significant' indicates that a chance difference as great as the one tested would occur in only .01 percent of an infinite number of cases.

[11] At least two manuscripts, Douce 321 and the source for Bodleian 788, have these texts arranged in parallel columns. In addition, one of the Gospel Sermons makes a topical allusion which is repeated in the Epistle group for a Sunday five weeks later. See *Select English Works,* I, xiii, n. 1; I, 137; and II, 302, n.a.

[12] There are approximately the same number of coordinating conjunctions per word in the two samples.
[13] "Wyclif's Prose", *Essays and Studies*, NS XIX (1966), 6.
[14] "Subordinate Clauses in Spoken and Written American English" (unpublished dissertation, used by permission of John Hanne, Communication Sciences Laboratory, University of Michigan [1964]), pp. 71-86. I have added information about the placement of the subject, verb, and object to his method of diagraming.
[15] Eyestone, "Subordinate Clauses", p. 86.
[16] The sentence reads: "And þerfore ȝiff it so be þat anny Cristen man be by a speciall grace of God preferred in dignite afore oþur, as Moyses, þat was choson prince of Goddes pepull, oþur þat anny man be more connynge oþur of more sotell consceyvynge þan oþur men ben, as Moyses was, þe wiche, as þe Maister of þe Stories seyþ in ys secound boke vppon scripture, seyþ þat he was a gret philosofre, ȝit I counceyll hym hoo þat he be not to be to inquisitiff how þat itt may be þat þe virginite and þe moderhed be bothe in Oure Lady, for þe cause her-of beþ not of common nature but of Goddes wurchynge and is hiȝe myracle and abowen þe common cours of kynde". *Middle English Sermons*, ed. Woodburn O. Ross (*EETS*, OS, 209) (London, 1940), p. 221-222.
[17] *Handbook of Middle English*, trans., James A. Walker (Baltimore, 1952), pp. 120-121.
[18] *The Works of Geoffrey Chaucer*, ed. Fred N. Robinson, 2nd ed. (Cambridge, Mass., 1957), pp. 322, 328.
[19] *Chaucer*, pp. 545-546.
[20] Hargreaves, "Wyclif's Prose", p. 11.
[21] Wyclif's contribution to the scholastic debate on the relation of God to time is found in *De Ente Praedicamentali, Latin Works*, XI, ed., R. Beer (Wyclif Society; London, 1891), 179-188 and in Sunday Epistle Sermon LV (II, 375).

7

THE MYSTI WITS: ALLEGORY AND METAPHOR

The New Testament is full of images, and any expositor who sets himself the task of explaining sections of it phrase by phrase is forced to explain the significance of parables, metaphors, and events which clearly have figurative implications. The learned preacher in the Middle Ages was able to choose from a vast collection of writings on the meaning of each of these figures, as well as exercise his own gift for exegesis. I am making a distinction here between allegory, which includes all interpretations of scripture which go beyond the literal texts, and metaphor, which describes those comparisons Wyclif himself creates between moral or spiritual teaching and the life around him.

It may surprise those of the "morning star of the Reformation" persuasion, that Wyclif knew and advocated in these simple English homilies Aquinas' four levels of Biblical interpretation: "It is seid comounly þat holy writt haþ foure undirstondingis. Þe first undirstondinge is pleyne, bi letter of þe storye. Þe secounde undirstondinge is clepid witt allegoric, whan men undirstonden bi witt of þe lettre, what þing shal falle here bifore þe dai of dome. Þe þridde undirstondinge is clepid tropologik, and it techiþ how men shudden lyve here in vertues. Þe fourþe undirstondinge is clepid anagogike, and it telliþ how it shal be wiþ men þat ben in hevene" (I, 30 also II, 277-8). He did not object to allegorical interpretation itself, only the misuses of it which neglect the literal level in favor of ingenious, learned glosses: "Þes wordis of Crist ben scorned of gramariens and devynes. Gramarians and filosophris seien, þat Crist knewe not his gendris; and bastard dyvynes seien algatis þat þes wordis of Crist ben false, and so no wordis of Crist bynden, but to þe witt þat gloseris tellen" (I, 376), and "here Anticristis tirauntis [the Church hierarchy] speken a$_3$en þe newe lawe, and seien þat literal witt of it shulde never be takun, but goostli witt; and þei feynen þis goostli witt after shrewid wille þat þei han" (II, 343).

Given these views, it should surprise no one that Wyclif begins his explication of the story of the calling of Peter with the identification of the fishermen's nets with "Goddis lawe" knitted with "four cardynale virtues", shaped to represent the "brook worldely lyf" gradually becoming narrower as the convert becomes "depid in Goddis lawe". Necessity for washing the net is the preacher's duty to proclaim God's word in the face of the dangers of man's law which "conteyneþ sharpe stones and trees, bi which þe nette of God is broken and fishes wenden out to þe world". The name of the River Genazereþ means "wounderful birþ", alluding to the second birth of the newly-won Christian soul (I, 13-14). This is the medieval allegorical tendency at work of course, but it must be contrasted with the rather pointless ingenuity of, for example, the writer of *Jacob's Well,* who identifies the sand in which Moses buried the Egyptian he killed with 'slugness' (p. 228), and urges the Christian to "delue depe wyth þi spade of clennesse in þis grond of lownesse tyl þou fynde þis spryng-watyr of grace, þat is, ȝyfte of pyte" (p. 252). Wyclif's interpretations are usually moral (tropologik) and are nearly always invited rather explicitly by the nature of the text. Christ does, after all call Peter to fish for men.

One medieval preacher, fascinated by the correspondence of various sets of numbers in the Bible, interprets Christ's feeding of the five thousand without, apparently, any thought of moral application. The lad figures Christ, in purity, truth, and kindness, the loaves are either the five wounds of Christ or the five stones with which David attacked Goliath, the two fish the Virgin and the penitent thief on the cross, and the twelve baskets left over either the twelve articles of the creed or the twelve Apostles.[2] Wyclif does not miss the chance to make identifications with all these wonderful numbers, but his emphasis is different *in kind* from the aimless associations of the other preacher. For him the five loaves are the five books of Moses, and the two fish the books of Wisdom and the prophets. In Wyclif's sermon the story becomes an analogy between bodily feeding and the spiritual nourishment Christ offered through his teaching of the books of the Old Law.

Nor do we find in Wyclif's 'mysti' interpretations the disregard for the sense and context of the passage displayed by John Bromyard in this explanation of a passage from Isaiah: corrupt lawyers choose ploughshares, "curved instruments, designed for earthly use and for temporal gain", instead of swords or spears, which are straight to signify impartiality, a complete reversal of the values given in the passage itself.[3] Even in the allegorizations which represent his furthest extremes Wyclif's correspondences may go beyond what modern exegesis could accept, but they do not go against the implications of the scripture. This is probably the result of his method of presenting and discussing the whole text for the day in each sermon, assuring that more than a single object or incident will occupy his attention.

There are also cases of less extended interpretation of items in the text with moral or doctrinal principles. These brief allusions are a compromise between allegorical interpretation and metaphor. Palsy is called a figure for instability of belief in Sermon XIX (I, 46-47), allowing the preacher to assert that Christ "helide mankynde of his goostly palesie", without further explanation. Similarly an allegorical reading of the parable of the prodigal son, which contrasts the father's good food with the hulls meant for swine, allows this succinct lesson to be drawn from the story: "For science of God fediþ men wel, and oþer science is mete for hoggis, and it makiþ men fat here, but not after domesdai" (II, 71). Perhaps the most striking use of this technique is Wyclif's interpretation of the parable of the good Samaritan (I, 31-33). The unfortunate traveller is Adam (and his descendents) who was beaten by the fiend and left wounded and unable to live a "just lyf". The Samaritan, Christ, treated the injuries with oil for healing and wine "to prik men fro synne". Then he "put mankynde upon his hors, whan he made his own manhede to be oure broþer and bere our syne". Unlike the dead-end identification of sand with slugness in *Jacob's Well,* Wyclif's method of allegorical reading allows the preachers who will use his outlines room for the extension and application required in a full-length sermon. Every identification nourishes a further revelation of doctrine or lesson in morality, and at the same time preserves the force and charm which the concreteness of the story should exert. This technique has a brilliant future in exegesis, as in John Donne's *Essays:* "Dig a little deeper, O my poor lazy soul, and thou shalt see that thou, and all mankind are delivered from an Egypt; and more miraculously than these".[4]

In addition to the treatment of the sermon text as a source of metaphor, Wyclif often employs Biblical concepts from other parts of the Bible for use as less extended images. The gospels are the commonest source for such figures, and of the gospel stories the most familiar is the identification of priests with shepherds (I, 201, 213, 230, 409; II, 254 and many more). Also frequent in these sermons is the figure of 'sour dow' (yeast) for hypocrisy. A *Commune Sanctorum* sermon interprets the image: "ri$_3$t as sour dow$_3$ shendiþ þe dow$_3$ þat it to longe dwelliþ wiþ, so synne of þese Pharisees shendiþ men þat consenten to it" (I, 223). There is elsewhere a reference to the unleavened bread of the exodus which Wyclif explains as the abandonment of old habits which cause new sins if they are not thoroughly cleansed (II, 286). Other occurrences of the figure seem to assume the reader's knowledge of these implications, as when, without explanation, Christians are warned to "beware wiþ sour dow of Pharisees" (I, 27, 57).

As in the recurring case of the Pharisees-friar equation, Wyclif often sets up analogies between New Testament life and that of his own time. The 'new sects' fast "as Joones disciplis; but Cristis disciplis taken noon hede but þat þei serve God wel" (II, 182). The device serves as a denunciation of the sects and at the same time an exhortation to right action. More commonly these analogies are used only as weapons against the sects, as when modern sellers of "chirchis bi symonye" are identified with those who sold doves in the temple at Jerusalem (II, 50), or the walls of Jerusalem shut against Christ with the cloisters "wallid a$_3$ens Cristen men" (I, 67). More arresting are these concise comparisons: "alle þes þree newe ordris comen not to þe þrittiþe greyn . . ." (II, 36), from the parable of the seeds; "þes ben þo þat God shittiþ out at domesday for defaulte of oile" (II, 312), from the story of the wise and foolish virgins; and "gidere up þe relief þat is lefte of Cristis mete" (II, 318), from the story of the loaves and fishes.

From the epistles come the familiar images of the Christians warfare against the devil and Christ's marriage to the Church. Several occurrences of these figures are unexceptional, but one or two go just far enough beyond the usual associations to be striking. For example, Christ is cited as "not bigamus" in his relation to the Church and as making "not dyvors" (I, 87, 88), and God's abandonment of the church is threatened because of her manifest "novelrye", leaving her "a widowe, forsaken of her spouse for her unkyndnes" (II, 301).

An evidence of the sustained interpretation of Old Testament events in the light of the New Testament are the images that claim the Christian convert supplants the devil "as Jacob dide Esau" (I, 114), and the printing of Christ's law in the people's souls was better than Moses printing of the decalogue on stones (II, 344). An extended discussion of the similarities of Christ's redemption to that of the golden adder which Moses held up, is begun in the gospel text itself, but it is notable for the great length to which Wyclif carries it (I, 161).

These briefer allusions show, I think, how thoroughly Wyclif's use of language was pervaded by the language of Scripture. But there are other vehicles for Wyclif's metaphor provided by other sources. Some images are based on special scientific knowledge. Wyclif was familiar with optics, and twice used little snatches of that science for metaphors. Spiritual vision is compared in one case with the heightened vision some men have in shade (II, 150) and in the other to seeing a penny in a dish only when it is covered with water (II, 299-300).[5]

From geometry come some observations on centers, "þe lowest of alle þingis" illustrative of meekness (I, 356, 399), of capacity to receive grace (I, 356), and of power to create order (I, 399). Straightness is also instructive, for "þe charite of Crist stretchiþ riȝtli wiþouten angle" (I, 273).

An extended discussion of the properties and causes of thunder teaches about the nature of spiritual enlightenment (I, 186). A great many lessons can be learned from the way a pearl grows inside an oyster, as the figure is changed from Christ as pearl in the shell of the world, to Christ as protective shell "stable and stef in all his temptaciouns", to his Godhead as an "unholid" pearl and his manhood as "hoolid, as shewen his fyve woundis" (I, 286). A similar discussion of the formation of salt reveals that it comes from gravel (the instability of the disciples at first), water (baptism), heat (charity), and wind (the Holy Ghost) (I, 267). As a result of the explanation of "erþe-denes" (earthquakes) we learn that as winds are closed inside the earth "so wyndis closid in proude preestis, and oþer men of þe world, ben figurid by erþe-dene" (I, 219). A text on watchfulness suggests the discussion of theories about sleep and their application to the spiritual sleep which is sin (I, 248-9). Although he specifically repudiates secular learning in itself, these instances of its employment in explaining the Bible show that Wyclif did both master and apply the insights of the sciences of his day.

The images from natural events which were matters of common observation also cover a range of subjects. The qualities of light make it and the sun and moon obvious subjects for moralizing. It is because of a special turn of the phrasing that Wyclif gets a singular effect: "a litil tyme, and sunne of ri3twisnesse is uppe" (II, 222), "þis is a greet synne to leve to ryse and open oure wyndowys; for þis spiritual li3t is redy to shyne to alle men þat wolen open" (II, 241), and "for ri3t as nestis in a sunne beem ben wel perceyved . . . so synnes ben wel perceyved of a man þat is in grace" (I, 277). The moon signifies Christ's manhood which is, like the moon, a second power (to his Godhood) (I, 108), and elsewhere the moon figures instability (II, 177).

Growing plants are used in various ways. The preacher often employs such images to reproach the sects as "moven gras þat were untedid", and destined to fade (II, 301), as boasters who say "þat þei ben erberis betir þan comoun pasture" (I, 28), and as roots of sin to be removed when Christ purges his congregation (I, 25). Wyclif warns his hearers that "as a 3erde mai growe so greet, and be so stiff in his strengþe, þat men shal not wriþe it, þou3 þei wolde never so fayn, so synne may growe in man . . ." (I, 278). The most memorable of these figures are: "For many wete someres ben comen to þe Chirche" and yet "mannis lawe growiþ and Goddis lawe is lettid" (I, 97), and "And bi þis þei swepten comynalte of men and maden hem bare and colde as floures ben maad" (I, 119).

Created nature "signefieþ" God as "smoke kyndely signefieþ fier" (I, 78), but the fire is better than the smoke and "þis halowyng þat last was figurid mut nedis be betir þan his figure" (II, 282). A similar preference of fire itself to smoke is implicit in "þei have fier of charite to make hem clere; for fumes of temporal goodis letten many to take þis spirit" (II, 307).

The doubting man is "unstable as þe water" and a flood of "þe see þat wiþ wynde is born aboute" (I, 53). Another passage compares those unstable ones who "fordiden soone Cristis prente" to those "stable as lond, þat helden þe prente þat Crist putt in hem" (I, 92). Concisely, man's law is "trobly water" (I, 14).

Jealousy and quarrelling among religious orders are to be expected, for "kynde techiþ þat ech beest loveþ beest like to him" (I, 57), not a great compliment as an ascription of motive. Unworthy preachers rob their parishoners as "þornes and bryres reven fro sheepe þer woole" (I, 21). Doves are like the active life, turtles the contemplative (I, 90). The saved perform the work of God, nor may they "turne as þe wynd . . ." (I, 21). Boasters "hav to mouche of sich wynd" (I, 408). John the Baptist was "groundid in þe stone of riȝt-wisnesse" (I, 72).

The images from nature forbid the conclusion that Wyclif's eyes were always on books. He must have retained some appreciation of the natural world or the range and perceptiveness of these metaphors would never have come to his mind. The denuded flower and the sheep's torn fleece must be seen before they can be turned to literary uses.

A few images depend on family life. The marriage relation or its perversion account for more than half of these. The elect of Christ shall be "knowun at domesday, bi clennes and bi bride cloþis" (II, 360), the church, led by wicked prelates, "is wydowe for þis tyme" (II, 187), and preachers who substitute man's lore for the gospel "put an hoore witt" for the true one and therefore "avoutren falsely Goddis word" (II, 217). The devil tempts men as "a lecchour seiþ to a womman þat he loveþ hir" (II, 314).

A man learning God's law must master the basic things first as "þis eire lernede first his a bi ce" (II, 239). The hand of God above mankind is like that of a "strong maistir and witti" whose "ȝerde were longe and shrape, reisid above þis childis heed" (II, 321). The patrimony of God is given equally to all his sons, yet Christ is "þe first eire" (II, 327).

Political organization supplies Wyclif with some comparisons. A natural image, often used in the Bible, is of spiritual and earthly kingship. Sometimes this takes the form of the greater seriousness of disobedience to God than to the king (II, 236), sometimes the pleasanter side of the greater worth of being the heir of heaven than the heir of a temporal kingdom (I, 402; II, 227). Through a slight shift in emphasis, if it is sinful to defoul a king's clothing, how much worse to cover truth with falsehood (I, 189). More sophisticated is the argument that Christ is present in the whole world in the same way that a king is simultaneously present in his whole realm (II, 142). The Christian is like a soldier serving under a captain (Christ) who wishes above all else to be commended to the king (God) (I, 196). Again, less explicitly, "Blessid be þis duke of bataile, þat þus rewardiþ his knyȝtis" (I, 344). The Church is armed with virtues as the castle is armed against enemies (I, 34).

From civil law come two figures. "God is trewe executour, and mai not faile to þee in goodis þat þou ȝyvest to him" (II, 40). The cautious Christian is like those advocates who "wolen no procure in a cause bifore þat þei heeren it, and þis cause to þer witt haþ þe part of riȝtwisnes" (I, 383), a rare case of the flattering mention of lawyers during the Middle Ages.

The images based on family and civil life do not convey disrespect for those customs. One would hardly conclude from them that Wyclif wished to destroy political loyalities or institute free love, as some of his older critics charged.[6]

Another large group of images is based on the faculties of the human body. Grounded in Scripture and abundant in medieval literature is the figure of Christ as physician, "hevenly leche" as Wyclif says (I, 7). Again, Christ healed mankind which "was born blynd, and sawe not þe grace of God" (II, 94). The duty of the priest is to diagnose spiritual illness as "a fisician lerneþ diligentli his signes, in veyne, in pows, and oþer þinges" (I, 151), and treat it effectively "as medecine shal be shapen aftir þat a syke man is disposid" (II, 330). For sometimes a man is so sick that he is "distempered fro good mete", and covets "þingis contrarie to his helþe", or lacks appetite completely, "a signe dedly to man, so wanting of Goddis witt is signe of his secounde deeþ" (I, 150). Nor would a reasonable man give a sword or knife to a "man in frenesie" (I, 26). A heretic is like a leper, who may infect all those among whom he dwells (I, 199).

Food is also the basis of several images. Although earthly food is savory at first and bitter as wormwood later, spiritual food becomes better and better, like spices when they are pounded (I, 89). The bread of the euchrist is chewed in the soul, hidden in the stomach, and nourishes "alle lymes of men, and turneþ man into God" (II, 82). Priests are the stomach of Christendom; if they are well and work vigorously, they can heal the whole body (II, 49). The new sects practice rules that "Cristis lawe haþ not defied [made ready]", so they are like meat that "makiþ mannis bodi to gurle [growl or gurgle]" (II, 249). Christians should be so virtuous that gossips have only good works to "gnawe upon" (II, 295). Some men are so hardened in their sin that they return like dogs to "eeten þe spuynge" (II, 330), and the new sects "grutchiden aȝens þis [Christ's] water, and drunken podel water of þe canel" (II, 335). Each part of the Church should act in accord with the others, "as partis of mannis bodi þat is hoole fiȝten not togidir, but raþer oon helpiþ anoþer, and kepiþ it fro many harmis" (I, 219), the truth "shulde have a synowe" (I, 47), and the fruit of a man's actions betrays his nature "as a child is ofte lyk to his fadir or to his modir" (I, 181). Only once does Wyclif echo the familiar medieval contempt of the body in his images: "but bodili fode is for þe bodi, and makiþ wormes mete redi" (I, 378).

An interesting feature of this group of figures is that they treat physical health as a good thing, although very much less good, of course, than spiritual well-being. On the other hand, they do not make an allurement of physical pleasure with an allegorical intent, as in the Song of Songs or some work of the medieval mystics.[7]

Other images are drawn from the common experience of anyone who was in touch with the land. Most refer to farming, domestic animals and tools. Several are governed by the general theme of the world as God's place of harvest. Thus, if the land will "bere good corn wiþouten tilyng and dongynge þerof", only a foolish man wastes his time doing those things (II, 299). The preacher must not let, for "defaute of preching, Goddis vynȝerde passe to a wortȝerd [vegetable garden]" (I, 331). To change the figure slightly, a man expects rewards in heaven as the "tiliyng man hopiþ ofte to have his fruyt" (I, 346), and should therefore cleanse his life "as men clensen lond of weedis; þei plucken hem up bi þe rootis" (II, 286). Evil men sometimes prosper on earth, much as the farmer allows "a bole þat shal be kild" to go "in corn at his wille" (I, 150).

The Jews must bear the burden of the old law as "assis beren chargis what so ever be leid on hem" (I, 66). The body should be looked after properly for it is "horse" to the soul (I, 263). Worldly love is no more charitable than "ȝif a man wolde fede a bridde, to take him aftir in þe granes [traps]" (II, 153). The modern Church offers assoiling for purchase, "as who so wolde bye an oxe or a cow" (I, 35). Highly paid priests are not good at warning secular men for "þe fend [devil] haþ stranglid þese houndis wiþ talwe, þat þei mai not berke" (I, 247). Sin makes one stumble as a blind horse who cannot recover his balance and eventually falls down (II, 352), or it binds one "as a bere to a stake" (II, 337). A similar image applies to the monks who are bound by their rule "as a bole bi a staake, to dwelle at hoom in cloistre" (II, 299). Prelates chase true apostles "as gre-houndis suen an hare" (II, 359), and make disunity in the Church like the "strif of doggis in a poke" (II, 358).

The man who consents to one sin, consents to all "as many men drawun a boot" (II, 202), and he who fails one neighbor fails all as if "many men bare a weiȝte" (II, 253). The truly meek man cooperates with God's will, for "God is a ferour [worker in iron]" and may make him a "hamer, or tongis, or a stiþie" (I, 407). Both John the Baptist (II, 2), and Paul (II, 240), are cited as God's whistles. Just as "bristil [needle] bryngiþ in þe þreed, and kynttiþ not þe leþer wiþinne, so Joones penaunce brouȝte Crist in, but Joon is not þe grace þat knittiþ" (II, 148). Truth is loose in us as nails in a tree "þerfore it is nedeful to knocke and make hem faste" (I, 70). Christ's order is a thong which binds men's wills together (I, 76), virtue a ladder by which we may reach the castle of heaven (II, 6), and love the spur to the women who visited Christ's tomb Easter morning (II, 145).

The sects are called lumps, first "lumpis of ypocritis" (II, 264), then, as apostles disobedient to Christ's command to wander in the world, they gather "in wete lumpis" (II, 301), and finally antichrist "stireþ hem togider, hepis of men of dyvers complexiouns" (II, 288). They are cruel toward faithful Christians, hitting them "as who shulde chulle a foot-balle" (II, 280), or striking them in the face until they "bollun [swell] unkyndly" (II, 261).

Money is mentioned in several metaphors. The man who trusts in the Pope's indulgences is like a rich man who tried to buy salvation and found himself the more severely damned (II, 318). As a great treasure contains many pennies, so one word of God contains many lessons (II, 253). "As false peny is noo peny, so fals reprofe is no repreefe" (I, 124). Christ offers man the chance to purchase heaven and "þis marchandiȝe shulde ech man do" (II, 221).

Again we must conclude that Wyclif was no stranger to the ordinary pursuits of laboring people, nor did he consider their problems too remote from God's message to be of illustrative value. G. R. Owst would include all of Wyclif's images among that "verbal illustration which describes everyday things as seen by the shrewd observer, and may be called 'realistic' ",[8] which is such an important bequest of the homilist to the world of English letters. Although he makes an impressive case for the constant use of such realism, Owst must draw from Latin as well as vernacular sources, and press into service hundreds of manuscripts, even then not reproducing the variety of the subject matter and treatment which may be found in Wyclif's five groups of short sermons, an observation which belies Henry Hargreaves comment that these sermons contain few comparisons.[9] Moreover, some of the examples Owst quotes did not originate with the "shrewd observer" in whose sermon they appear—they came from books. Such a case is the extended analogy of laundering, found in no. 42 of *Middle English Sermons,* but existing in both English and French analogues dating from the twelfth century.[10] These considerations do not, of course, damage Owst's excellent case for the influence of preaching on later literature, for even if all preachers did not achieve great variety or originality in their metaphors, they assuredly kept the "realistic" method alive. Nevertheless it belongs to Wyclif's sermons to display *par excellence* the temper of the preacher who "had direct and continuous contact with Life",[11] and set the common things of daily life "high amid the wider concerns of the human mind, thus making their dust fat with fatness".[12]

A second feature of Wyclif's metaphors is their explicitness. Again, this is not an exclusive mark of Wyclif's style, but a fairly common property among preachers. It does serve to separate him from the prose tradition of the mystics, however, whose figures are often mood-evoking and elusive as in the extended image of the cloud in *The Cloud of Unknowing.*[13]

A third characteristic of the images in these sermons is their brevity. The only metaphors which supply more than a sentence are those whose terms come from Scripture. The one-page discussions of thunder (I, 186-7), pearls (I, 286), and salt (I, 267-8), are begun by the text, although a mass of medieval learning which helps supply their 'mysti' interpretations is appended to the simple references of the Bible. His own metaphors Wyclif never treats so fully. There is good reason for noting this distinction, for while in theory at least, the words of Scripture might contain all four kinds of spiritual truth, the figures designed by the preacher himself have a much more limited use.[14]

Sometimes, but rather rarely, an image is established explicitly early in the sermon, abandoned, and then brought back by a word or phrase later on. For example, worldly goods and temporal power are the two 'brondis' that keep the pot of strife in the clergy boiling. Later comes the accusation that those who say they wish the Church cleansed of sin nevertheless "putte under fier, and leve [fail] to wiþdrawe þe brondis" (II, 202). The same technique is used with images established in the Scriptural text and repeated later as, "*He shal not breke a rede . . . and he shal not quenche flex þat smokiþ, til he caste out juginge to victorie*". Later, "he was meke to seculers here, þat weren unstable as þe reed, and meke to preestis of þe chirche, þat smokiden bi pride as brent flex" (II, 189).

Sometimes the literal point is made, and the figure merely used to strengthen it. Thus the tongues of Pentecost resulted when the apostles spoke in their own language and were understood by each listener in his own language, "as þe same sound of bellis moveþ men diverseli, oon þat þei speken þus, anoþer þat þei speken dyvers" (II, 307). Occasionally the metaphoric statement becomes a sort of epigram as, "As false peny is noo peny, so fals reprofe is no repreefe" (I, 124). It may have the ring of a watch word, as "sunne of ri$_3$twisnesse is uppe" (II, 222). Sometimes a whole atmosphere is created by a single figurative word, inserted in an otherwise literal sentence. References to "God's whistles" work this way, as does a mention of our hope for defeat of the "fend" "bi sparclis of grace þat we felen" (I, 279).[15]

By its 'realism', its explicitness, and its brevity, Wyclif's imagery performs several services for his prose style. It blunts the abstractness of a sermon method which specifically excludes non-Biblical narratives. It establishes a bond, also suggested in the diction of the sermons, between the lessons of holy Scripture and the matter of the people's lives. It teaches doctrine where the official language of dogma would necessarily fall far short. It insults with a precision and vividness which no general statement could carry. And occasionally, as with the 'torn fleeces' of sheep and the 'sparklis' of grace, it warms the heart.

[1] Ed. Arthur Brandeis (*EETS*, OS, 115) (London, 1900).

[2] See G. R. Owst, *Literature and the Pulpit in Medieval England* (Cambridge, England, 1933), p. 62.

[3] Owst, *Literature*, p. 63.

[4] Ed. Evelyn M. Simpson (Oxford, 1952), p. 74.

[5] An extended discussion of light refraction is found in *Sermones, Latin Works* VI, ed. Johan Loserth (London, 1890), Part II, 388.

[6] For example, Joseph Stevenson, S. J., *The Truth About John Wyclif* (London, 1885), p. 143.

[7] See H. O. Taylor, *The Medieval Mind* (Cambridge, Mass., 1925), especially on St. Bernard, vol. I, ch. VI, and vol. II, ch. XXXVII, and on the women mystics, vol. I, ch. XXV.

[8] *Literature*, p. 23.

[9] "Wyclif's Prose", *Essays and Studies*, NS XIX (1966), p. 16.

[10] Ed. Woodburn O. Ross (*EETS*, OS, 209) (London, 1940), p. 247.

[11] Owst, *Literature*, p. 55.

[12] Owst, *Literature,* p. 46.
[13] Ed. Phyllis Hodgson (*EETS,* OS, 218) (London, 1874-93).
[14] Later preachers, John Donne, for example, and Jonathan Edwards, develop their non-Scriptural metaphors as fully as those they find in the Bible, in some cases attributing to them the equivalent of the four medieval allegorical senses.
[15] A similar image appears in *The Cloud of Unknowing,* p. 22, where the author describes certain impulses of the soul as "speedly springing unto God as sparcle fro þe cole".

8

THE MEDIEVAL MIND: SCHOLASTICISM AND FOLKLORE

So far the prose techniques of these sermons have revealed an author with a radical idea, an idea which not only coordinated Wyclif's thought on most subjects, but also influenced his habits of expression and perhaps his habits of conception as well. A great deal of Wyclif is revealed by following his theory of the availability of God's grace through the Bible backward to its source in philosophical realism and forward to its implications for practical reform. It took him, in Miss Deanesly's phrase 'very far',[1] far toward personal danger, and, from our point of view, far toward modern Protestantism. But this view of Wyclif, as long as it remains unqualified, fails to clarify much of what is valuable and attractive in his preaching style. For the real significance of the English prose is not that Wyclif could write modern English, but that he could embody a radical, modern idea in a language and an aura of thought which pulled him from at least two directions back into something medieval.

Defining what is medieval in Wyclif's style implies that medievalism itself has been defined. Rather than attempt the synthesis of a huge body of commentary on the general subject, my approach will be to describe Wyclif's 'medievalism' in terms of two institutions which almost all scholars, I think, will agree belong distinctively to the Middle Ages. The first is formal scholasticism and the second is the popular pulpit. These two expressions of the medieval manner of thinking have the additional value of being the two disciplines most directly relevant to Wyclif's plans for sermon construction.

It is not the subject matter of scholastic argument which is of particular concern here, although it is certainly true that Wyclif arrived at his theological position by considering the traditional and central problem of medieval philosophy–the problem of knowledge.[2] It is the method of scholastic debate, and the mutations of that method in Wyclif's sermons, which have such interesting implications for his style as a preacher. The apparatus of the schools itself changed, of course, through the centuries of its importance, but it may be fairly characterized as involving the division of a question, the citation of authority concerning each division, and the resolution of the question according to reason (i.e., logic). In the hands of the best scholastic writers the method yielded much insight, but by the mid-fourteenth century the machinery had become too cumbersome for its waning inspiration. It was a time "when logic had ceased to act as a stimulant to the intellectual powers and had become rather a clog upon their exercise, and when men no longer framed syllogisms to develop their thoughts, but argued first and thought, if at all, afterwards".[3] Wyclif's Latin treatises afford several examples of absurdly delicate argumentative machinery given over to what could not possibly have been a serious search for truth. It is disappointing to see our sensible preacher trying to prove an assertion about confession from a quibble about the gender of *solus*.[4] On the other hand, the mastery Wyclif displays of the methods of scholastic thought deepens our appreciation of his adaptation to the prose techniques of the English sermons; the more impressive is this shift when we realize how great a residue of the thinking of the schools inheres in the sermons. The simplicity of Wyclif's reference to the appearance of a penny in a dish (II, 299-300), is more remarkable when written by a man able to discourse at length on direct, reflected, and refracted rays of light and to perceive in these three modes of light transmission three corresponding rays of love.[5]

The English sermons never utilize the three steps of scholastic debate as they were used for formal argument at Oxford; Wyclif's method of sentence by sentence textual exegesis will not allow that. Traces of each of the three used separately, however, appear as the techniques of subdivision, authority, and formal logic.

A scholastic interest in orderly subdivision suggests that there should be four kinds of greatness involved in the words of Christ's parable "*þere was a man þat makide a greet soper* . . ." (I, 4), and five causes why "*dyverse folkis*" came to hear Jesus preach, analogous to the five places from which they came (I, 214), and to the five Old Testament sins (II, 333-335). The great weight of interpretation accumulated through centuries rested on any learned medieval preacher, even though he himself may only have sampled the Fathers through the glosses; for a scholar of Wyclif's scope and depth it must have rested heavily. The tendency to subdivide ordinary assertions like these are evidences of that weight. Other *divisios* simply elaborate or number the items of the text, as in the enumeration of the sixteen conditions of true charity from I Corinthians 13 (II, 266-268), the twenty-seven gifts of God to his servants, from Romans XII (II, 246-249), the twelve fruits of a merciful spirit, from Colosians III (II, 255), the eight virtues recommended by Peter in I Peter III (II, 325-327), and the seventeen works of the flesh and the twelve fruits of the spirit suggested by Galations V (II, 348). In these cases the divisions are a mere convenience for explaining the text and perhaps an aid for the listeners' memories. In other (rare) passages, however, not the text, but the glosses of the 'clerkis', provide the items of the division. The four endowments of Christ's glorified body (subtlety, agility, incorruptibility, and transparency) and of his soul (knowledge, capacity, nimbleness, and subtlety) (I, 142-143 and II, 234-235), is one of few such cases. There is no mention anywhere in these sermons of the seven deadly sins, although there is one hint that Wyclif had the elaborate classification of sins in mind when he called hypocricy "þe firste spice of pride" (I, 27).

Even in passages which seem to follow the text with singular fidelity, the habit of division is apparent. When Ephesians IV, 23 says "*þat men shulden cloþe þe newe man þat is born aftir God in riȝt hoolynesse and truþe*", the preacher points out the traditional correspondence between each virtue and one member of the Trinity, "riȝtwisnes" to the Father, "holynes" to the Son, and "treuþe" to the Holy Spirit (II, 361). So casual are passages like this one that it is reasonable to assume that they arise from a habit of thought, at one time carefully learned of course, but by the time of the writing of these sermons almost unconscious.

There is another facet to the *divisio* technique–medieval numerology. While many of the classifications place no stress on the number of items involved, some make the number itself into a unit of significance. Five thousand men will be saved by the spiritual food of the miracle of the loaves and fishes "for fyve is a round nombre þat turneþ wiþouten eende in to him silf" (I, 121), and the virgins attending the wedding are five foolish and five wise, "for þe wise shal be in hevene evere in a sercle of blisse, as fyve is noumbre in a sercle; and þe toþer five foolis shal be dampned in helle wiþouten eende" (I, 290). Both these interpretations of the number refer to its roundness[6] and extend roundness to imply eternality. Two is twice cited as the symbol of imperfection, since it is "þe first noumbre þat partiþ fro unite" (I, 18, 63). In a sermon on the nativity the number seven is introduced almost gratuitously, for it adds less to the listener's grasp of Christ's seven virtues (only cited as three of the body, three of the soul, and his Godhead) than of the meaning of seven itself. "And so, as sevene is ful nombre of universite of þingis, so Crist is ful rewme of hevene, and of þis world" (I, 320). The number of elders prophesied in the Apocalypse has an ingenious, but opaque, significance: "For riȝt as foure tymes sixe maken þis noumbre, so foure wittis of holy writt, þat is perfit, maken þes eldir men" (II, 309).

Just as casual as the subdivision of ideas in the text, and much more frequent, is the citation of authority. Specific references are never given. Where a preacher of the 'modern' persuasion gives an exact account of the book and chapter he is quoting,[7] Wyclif introduces his quotations with, "As Austin seiþ" (II, 225), or "þus seiþ Bernard" (II, 318). Often he even phrases his citations to mark his approval, "herfore seiþ Austin wele" (II, 235), and "as Austin declariþ wel" (II, 285), which practice would seem to imply that even Augustine might be trusted on some points more confidently than on others (but nowhere in these sermons does he find his master wanting). The Fathers themselves are never the point of departure for extended reasoning; they are introduced to support a proposition already established from the text. The proper uses of Patristic authority are suggested by Wyclif in his interpretation of the miracle of the feeding of the five thousand. The loaves and fishes represent the learning of the Old Testament which Christ gave directly to the people; the "berlepis [carrying baskets] of relif ben alle þe sentences of seintis after, bi which þei feden trewe men by delyng of Goddis lawe" (I, 19). This, by the way, supports Gordon Leff's assertion that Wyclif did not teach 'scriptura sola'.[8]

His choice of authorities confirms an opinion of Wyclif as a conservative theologian. The Bible is cited more than four and a half times as often as the next most frequent authority (Augustine), not counting references to the text from which Wyclif is preaching.[9] Augustine is cited almost thirty times, and seems to have been the last man Wyclif would wish to disregard or controvert. This allegiance places him squarely in the center of medieval practice, for nearly every philosopher of the scholastic period counted himself a disciple of Augustine, each taking his point of departure from a different facet of Augustine's rich legacy of thought.[10] Gregory is cited eight times, Ambrose four, and Nicholas de Lira three. Bernard and Grosseteste are each mentioned twice, and Bede, Josephus, Anselm, Isidore, Origen, and Chrysostom once. It is significant that the only 'modern' authorities are de Lira, who is never mentioned by name but merely used as the source for legends, and Grosseteste, to whom Wyclif was singularly indebted in several ways. Aristotle is cited for a logical principle in two passages, but a third disclaims the appropriateness of his authority in doctrinal matters: "And þis Baptist was a witnesse more worþ þan þes philosophris, as Plato and Aristotle, boþe in liif and in witt" (II, 5). There are scores of references to 'clerkis', 'heretikes', or 'Pelagians'[11], which contain no quotations, but merely unflattering paraphrases.

The English sermons are not designed to debate abstruse theology but to instruct and inspire a rural congregation; yet in certain doctrinal matters their author's taste for formal argument cannot always be subordinated to his stated aims. One form such argumentation takes is the presentation of alternative solutions to a question, resulting in an acceptance or rejection of the premise on which both are based. The irresistibility of God's will is debated by Wyclif much as it was by Bradwardine in *De Causa Dei* forty years before:[12] "if a man do meedfulli þat God biddiþ him do, Goddis wille is ri$_3$tli fillid in deed . . . $_3$if a man a$_3$enstondiþ God and doiþ a$_3$ens his wille, $_3$it Goddis wille is fillid asideli by punishinge of þis man" (I, 324, also II, 33). The passage continues with corroboration from "Latyn", which may be *De Causa Dei*. In the sermon text *Imitatores mei estote* (Phil. III, 17), Paul asks the Philipians to follow him "in werks and lyf", and Wyclif shows that simoniac prelates are unable to avoid logical contradiction, the mark of the devil: "ech synne of þe fend is contrarie to himsilf" (II, 371).

A classic case of the technique of *reductio ad absurdum* is used to affirm the utter reliability of God's words in the Bible. The disbeliever might as well say "bi þe same skile [for the same reason]" that "God were þe falseste þing þat evere was in þis world. For þei seien þat falshede is no defaulte in a þing whi seien þei not þat God is fals for perfeccioun of God . . . For, siþ falshede in God is good, ȝeve we him ynowȝ þerof; for God mai not have a name, but ȝif he passe al oþer þing" (I, 369-370). The conclusion is so obvious that the preacher closes his sermon, "Blessid be treuþe, þat made us passe alle sich fantasies . . ." rather than give a further refutation of the error.

Another resource of formal logic is employed in his answer to those "heretikes" who argue that "ȝif God biddiþ þat Y shal love my frend, he biddiþ bi contrarie witt þat Y shal hate myn enemye". In this case, unlike the previous examples, even the terminology of the schools remains in the reply: "But þes foolis knewen not þat þis sueþ al oonli whanne antesedent and consequent ben convertiblis in kynde" (II, 41). Instead of explaining the terms, the preacher shifts the whole argument to more homely ground by pointing out the dangers of hating and the values of loving.

Formal syllogism appears, but very rarely. On Luke XI, 27, *"blessid be þei þat heeren Goddis word and kepen it"*, Wyclif forms this neat dismissal of friars' letters of fraternity "Heryng and kepyng of Goddis word is betere þan þe birþe of Crist; þis birþe is betere þan þes lettris, and so heeryng and kepyng of Goddis word is algatis betere þan þes lettris" (I, 380).

The verbal quibble, which unfortunately also represents late scholasticism, is attacked in one of these sermons. The literal argument is put in the mouth of Antichrist who "grutchid" against the text *"Lo daies comen, seiþ þe Lord, and Y shal rere up David . . ."* He boasts "þat he can prove þat þer ben not many tymes, and how shulden þanne daies come? where daies han feet for to go?" (II, 375). Wyclif, then can sweep away such trivia by a serious treatment of the relation of time to God.

One scholastic technique used here rather often is specifically associated with preaching rather than argumentation in general, and may employ all sorts of logical devices in its manipulation. It is the settling of dubious points of the text,[13] and typically, Wyclif must have an imaginary opponent to raise the questions. Sometimes Antichrist, as in the last example, sometimes the new sects, or the friars specifically, serve as mouthpieces for the rejected case, but most often the doubt is presented simply by 'men'. Thus "here men axen comunly, whi Jesus, þat is almyȝty, helide not first fulli þis man . . ." (II, 193), gives occasion to the preacher to attach meaning to the exact actions of Christ in the incident. The practice of the Greek Church is used to raise a doctrinal issue, and Wyclif is willing to leave its position intact because "oþer pointis weren now more nedeful to þe Chirche" (I, 152). Several explanations are given to settle doubts about the number of kings who worshipped the child Jesus (II, 243), and even the disposal of food by Christ's resurrected body is made the subject of a "disputed question"—the food was, by the way, "avoidid on honest maner" (II, 137). A more fundamental issue is raised when Wyclif argues against "þes heretikes" who base their theology on the utter unpredictability of God's will, following the theory of William of Occam (II, 235).

Digression does not belong to scholasticism more than to other disciplines, but particular digressions were especially common among its latter-day practitioners. Frequently the Eucharist became the subject of digressions; Wyclif often mentions it whether he has textual warrant or not. In an extreme example the matter appears in a completely unrelated discussion: "þanne men shulden heere Goddis word gladly, and dispise fablis, and erre not in þis sacrid oost, but graunte þat it is two þingis, boþe breed and Goddis body,–but principaly Goddis bodi. And certis he þat dispisiþ þe prechoure whan he prechiþ Goddis wordis, dispisiþ boþe God and man" (II, 274). Even more abrupt is this brief digression on the Eucharist: "Joon is not Hely personali, as Joon him silf confessiþ; but he is Hely figurali, as Crist seiþ here, þat mai not lye. And riȝt so þe sacrid oost is verry breed kyndeli, and Goddis bodi figurali, riȝt as Crist himsilf seiþ. And, for þis witt is notable, Crist seiþ, as he seiþ ofte, *He þat haþ eeren to heere, heere he* . . ." (II, 6). These brief allusions occur very often and hint at the constant presence of this subject in Wyclif's mind.

Although in general Wyclif did not approve of "curiouste of science or unskilful coveitise of cunnyng" (I, 227), there are a few subjects to which he brings learning in biology or optics. Speculation about the soul of an embryo is a case in point; the preacher concludes that John the Baptist must have been conceived before Christ because he made "joie in mannere of dansing" when Mary told Elizabeth of the conception of Jesus. Wyclif warns against the belief that "it is six moneþis bifore þat þe soule be couplid wiþ þe bodi, and bifore it haþ plantid [vegetable] soule,[14] and siþ soule of beeste" (I, 369). Behind this brief remark lies the learning of Augustine and Aquinas, who, like Wyclif, dispute the contention that the soul of a babe before birth passed through vegetable and animal stages (I, 369, n. 1). The refutation is given, without apology or explanation, the basis of Scriptural truth alone "but as we bileven þe wordis of þe gospel". The source of a "lunatike's" illness is the "movyng of þe moone", and the symptoms of paralytics are that "þei mai not riȝtli move þer partis for feblenesse of þer senewis" (II, 23).

Christ's admonition to his disciples to be the light of the world is the occasion for a discussion of the properties of light, its spirituality, generality, orderliness, and effect of giving comfort to man. Each quality implies a corresponding duty for the modern disciple (I, 269). Learning which arises from Scripture (like that which these examples display) and which is guided by the impulse to teach God's will is helpful to the preacher: "oþer science is mete for hoggis" (II, 71). Twice optics supplies the vehicle for Wyclif's metaphors. Spiritual vision is compared in one case with the heightened vision some men have in shade (II, 150), and in the other to seeing a penny in a dish only when it is covered with water (II, 299-300).

The contribution of the popular pulpit to our understanding of medievalism defines a pole exactly opposite the abstraction of scholasticism. The beginner in religious experience, according to Evelyn Underhill, "finds a difficulty about universals, and is most at home with particulars". He singles out a "special saint, or even a local form of the Madonna".[15] The attraction of pictures and statues of the saints and of graphic accounts of their stories was carefully valued by spokesmen of the church,[16] and the instructive autobiography of Margery Kempe shows that at least for some lay people the appeal of such particulars was strong.[17] The friars' instruction books found ample space, not only for saints' lives, but for stories of devils and witches and their dealings with men. It was that sort of thing, rather than a disquisition on the Trinity or freedom of the will, which engaged the hearts and stabilized the loyalities of the ordinary people. Even if Owst is correct in observing that legends like those of John Mirk only baptised the deities of a pre-Christian era,[18] the fact remains that the folk imagination was able to grasp these grotesque personages and revere them as it could not the conceptual forces of the scholars.

Because he specifically repudiated the use of any non-Biblical narratives in preaching, Wyclif set himself a more than usually difficult task. The resources of classical or pagan myth and of English folk-lore were alike closed to him. Yet he needed to arouse in his hearers a zeal so strong that it would withstand the displeasure of the visible Church.

Wyclif rarely recounts the stories of saints or the unScriptural traditions about Biblical characters and objects which so intrigued the late medieval audience. Once he refers to Saint Margaret, who was a special favorite in England, but only a brief hint is given of her story, in that she, with many other saints, could hold dragon-shaped fiends against their wills. The real point shifts quickly to the moral lesson Christ intended by his injunction to overcome evil spirits (I, 187-88). Twice Wyclif mentions legends found in Nicholas de Lira's writings (I, 86, II, 56). The first is the tradition that John the Baptist was the bridegroom at the marriage in Cana for which Christ miraculously supplied wine. Wyclif cites the myth only to dismiss it with, "Studie we not to what woman þis Joon was weddid, ne axe we not autorite to prove þat Joon was weddid now; ffor þat þe gospel seiþ here is ynow to Cristen feiþ" (I, 86). Perhaps he introduces it in order to dismiss it. The other legend concerns the healing powers of the water from which the tree for Christ's cross had grown. Again the story is not just deemphasized, it is deliberately set apart from the textual exegesis: "But leeve we þis bineþe bileve, and stonde we in wordis of þis gospel" (II, 56).

The appeal to folk imagination through demonology has a long and highly developed history among medieval writers. There is no question that Wyclif believed in the powers of the devil and his emissaries; the amazing thing is that he did not depict them oftener and in more affective language. We can neither prove nor disprove, says Wyclif, statements about "elves and sum gobelyns", but it is

> "licly þat þes fendis have power to make boþe wynd and reyne, þundir and liȝtyng, and oþer wedir; for whan þei moven partis of þis erþe, and bringen hem nyȝ togidere, þes partis moten nedly bi kynde maken siche werdis . . . Al þes fendis han witt and power to move mennis hertis and oþer lymes, aftir þat þei gessen men to be temptid to a goostli synne"

The attributions of power are accompanied by a classification of the various levels of fiendishness. Even in such a detailed passage, however, there seems to be no attempt to render the devils imaginable. Wyclif gives his reason–it is the same as before: "hold we us in bondis þat God telliþ in his lawe" (II, 366).

There was another approach to the problem of making Christianity available, as it were, to the imagination. Medieval preachers often dramatized and updated the Bible stories themselves. Scriptural figures appear in feudal guises; in Mirk, for example, Potiphar is "mastyr of the kyngys knyghtys", and "Pilate, Herod's lefetenant, undyr hym, of all his lond of Jury".[19] Sermon 39 of the *Middle English Sermons* speaks of the magi as if they were Oxford scholars in orders (p. 226). Sometimes the Bible stories were actually distorted in their transformation to an English medieval setting, but often they took on a vivid and homely reality.

Wyclif takes very few liberties with his text, but he does translate some details: the centurion is a "litil kyng" (I, 52), the disciples, Christ's "kynȝtis" (II, 342), and Bethlehem not "þe kingis citiee", but a "pore uplondish toun" (I, 341). Christ was able to perform "more wondirful werkes þan men don in somer games" (II, 23). The performance of Salome before Herod's court is "tumbleris lepyng" (I, 388), and John the Baptist was authorized to baptize because he was a "hooli prophete and a bishopis sone" (II, 5). The nativity scene is envisioned with touching reality: Christ lay "bifore an oxe and an asse. And breeþ of þes two beestis kepte him hoot in þis cold tyme" (I, 317). In a scathing rebuke to the monks, Wyclif shows the same ability to bring the Biblical scene into the common idiom: "Crist clepide not þes two apostlis to his chaumbre to ete applis, but in þe comun feld, he clepide hem fro worldli traveil, and tolde hem of a betere traveile" (I, 301-302).

A commoner technique in Wyclif's sermons is to present the Biblical text with little adornment, but to color and dramatize the modern practice with which he wishes to contrast it. For example, it is not the words or the situation of Christ when he says "*I seie to ȝou, þat ech man þat seeþ a womman and coveitiþ hir, to synne wiþ hir, is now lecchour in his soul*" which is particularized, it is those modern men who "speken wiþ wymmen of hevene, of vertues, and good þing, and ȝit disposyng dwelliþ in hem to make hem þenke amys aftir" (II, 175); not the ten virgins carrying oil (the oil of devotion) for the wedding, but the modern friars who represent the foolish in their lack of spirituality and "taken her stait to lyve lustli in þis world, for ellis þei shulden be laborers, and lyve hard lyf in lewid stait" (I, 292).

Folk wisdom, although more common in other vernacular sermon-writers, finds a small place in these sermons. When Wyclif asserts that sin "bringiþ man to fyve markis more noyousli þan oþer skilis" (I, 370), he is apparently quoting part of a proverb on poverty, and he ascribes to "þe poete" a proverb in which "þe frogge seide to þe harwe, cursid be so many lordis" (II, 280). A bit of folk wisdom is reflected in his view of women "where þei ben goode, passen oþer creaturis, so, where þei ben turned to yvel, þei passen many oþer fendis" (I, 388), and monks are helpless "out of þer cloistre as fishis wiþouten water" (II, 15), in Wyclif as well as Chaucer.

I have placed the abstraction of scholasticism and the concreteness of the popular pulpit at opposite poles. Like all polar opposites, they must be sustained by a single continuum, in this case a philosophical idea. The medieval world view asserts the meaningfulness of every aspect of the universe because of its revelation of the plan of God for natural phenomena and for a human moral order. It results in the theological use of natural science, etymology, and history. An integral part of Platonic and scholastic thought, the idea is nevertheless translatable into the homeliest folk tales of the medieval pulpit and hearth. It sustains at the same time Anselm's ontological proofs of God's existence and the allegorical meanings of the jointlessness of elephants' knees.

The precise manner in which Wyclif espoused this fundamental scholastic debate is discussed fully by Professor Leff in *Heresy in the Later Middle Ages,*[20] but it is highly significant that as a vernacular preacher Wyclif not only used the notion, as it was impossible to avoid doing, but recognized and stated it, in simple terms, within the sermons: "And certis, siþ þat God wiste, ȝhe, bifore he made þis world, þat Abraham shulde be, þanne it was soþ, and herfore seyen clerkes þat ech creature haþ beyng in his sample þat is wiþouten eende" (I, 127). Everything extant has simultaneous and eternal existence in the mind of God, and therefore nothing is without plan and meaning for men, who, of course, must fulfill their part of that order. The World in a Grain of Sand which Blake's extraordinary vision enabled him to see, was Wyclif's constant environment.

Many techniques which have already been discussed exemplify the application of this idea to the most minute matters of both scripture and the natural world. I would like to add a few more, as token representatives of the enormous importance of the habit of mind which is, as C. S. Baldwin says, a mode of conception rather than expression only.[21] "For kynde haþ ȝovun to men to heeren voicis in þe eire, and not in erþe bineþen us, where voices comen not; in tokne þat we shulden ȝyve oure wittis to trowe þing þat mai be in eire, þat is aboven us, which þing profitiþ to oure soule" (I, 250-251). The same thought informs his concept of the relation of events to time: "þingis þat moven kyndely, moven faster toward þe eende" (II, 222), suggests that the ages of history are rushing toward doomsday with a speed which behooves men to repent.

All the bestiaries which offered moralizations for their natural wonders must have operated on this principle. Wyclif includes a very few discussions of the habits of animals, and then only when his text makes it necessary. Yet the lore is there to be exploited, as in the case of the serpent and dove in Matthew IX.

> "An eddre haþ þis witt; whanne charmeris come to take him, þe toon of hise eeris he clappiþ to þe erþe, and wiþ þe eende of his tail he stoppiþ þe toþer. And so Goddis children, whanne þei be temptid to synne, þei þenken mekeli how freel þei ben maid of þe erþe, and wiþ greet þouȝt of her deþ, þat shal come, þei witen not whanne, and drede of her jugement lest þei he demyd to helle, þei stoppen her oþer eere and kepen hem wel fro synne "

The innocence of the dove, who has no claws for defense, leads her to,

> "tristen not to her owne strengþe, but fallen on stones, and þese haukis dreden þanne to smyte at hem, lest þei frushen her owne brest at þe hard stoone. So Cristis disciplis knowen mekeli her freelti, and liȝten on þe corner stoon, þat is Jesus Crist; and þanne fendis of helle dreden hem to swippen at hem, lest þei harmen hem silf at þe stoone of hurtinge" (I, 201)

The sheep and wolves of John X, 11, however, are given no characteristics beyond those suggested in the text (I, 138-140).

Language, although a human institution, is also amenable to treatment as minutely revealing of God's will. The popularity of etymological proofs is found in the most learned and the simplest sermons alike. The very words of the Bible, even though those words were the Latin of Jerome rather than the Hebrew and Greek of the original inspiration, were revered and glossed as significant in themselves. It is probably the force of that view of interpretation which prompted Wyclif to make his first version a 'construe'. Not until the Renaissance was what W. Schwarz calls a philological view of translation of the Bible at all widely acknowledged.[22]

Etymology, then, became more than a way of introducing an idea or assisting the hearer's memory, it assumed the role of evidence. The meaning of 'Canaan' (changed or changing) confirms the lesson to be learned from the conversion of the Canaanite woman (I, 115), and the interpretations of 'Chana' and 'Galilee' as "gelousnes" and "a turning wheel" help the allegory provided by Christ's first miracle (I, 88). Sometimes whole itineraries are interpreted in this way. From the text "*Jesus went oute of þe contree of Tirus and he cam by Sidoun to þe water of Galile*" (Mark VII, 31), Wyclif makes this analysis. Jesus began at Tirus, which is 'makynge' to signify that he "wente fro þe bosim of þe fadir of hevene . . . God made of noȝt boþe aungels and men and al þis brood worlde", he passed through Sidon "þat is angel kynd", when he greeted Mary through the angel Gabriel, and healed man's breech with God, for Sidon is also 'helþe', finally he went to Galilee "a wheel whirlinge or passinge" to signify his assumption of man's fallen state (I, 29-30). The victim on his way from Jerusalem to Jericho in the parable of the Good Samaritan was, as an analogue of Adam and Eve, leaving the "siȝt of pees" for the "state of slydyng" (I, 32). The nobleman ("litil kyng") who came up from Capharnaum was leaving a "feld of fatnesse; for man fattid and alardid wendiþ awey fro God", and accepting Galilee, "transmigracioun", for he "mette wiþ Jesus in playn weie, and lefte his heþene possessioun, and preide God . . ." (I, 52).

The etymologies are not always, or even usually, philologically sound; they come from the tradition of the glossators rather than from Wyclif's own research in Hebrew and Greek. (In fact, Wyclif probably knew no Hebrew and very little Greek)[23] He therefore offers "strong bi his hond" as a meaning of 'David' (II, 375), derives August (Caesar Augustus) from *augeo* "for he alargide þe empire" (I, 316), and considers 'Tiberius' to refer to the river Tiber, for, like it, the man was "unstable as watir" (II, 10).

What is clear from language, in the medieval view, is equally clear from history. Following the exegetical method of the Fathers, Wyclif posits a close and literal revelation of the New Testament in the Old. Again the underlying idea is the pattern which existed in the mind of God from the beginning of time, and which becomes gradually more and more fully revealed by the process of history. There are two aspects of this view of events, both amply illustrated in the sermons. The first is the prefiguring of the New Testament in the Old and the second the prefiguring of the fourteenth century in the New Testament. The first corresponds to the definition St. Thomas and Wyclif himself give to the allegorical sense of Scripture "so far as the things of the Old Law signify the things of the New Law", and the second to his definition of the moral sense "so far as the things done in Christ, or so far as the things which signify Christ, are types of what we ought to do".[24]

Wyclif's attention to the relationship between the old and new laws is authorized by the beginning of the Gospel of Mark which he interprets as an indication of "how Crist was teld in þe olde lawe, and how al his lyf was figurid boþ in patriarkis and prophetis" (II, 2). Again in a later sermon he writes "al þat fel in þe oolde law was figure of Jesus Crist" (II, 8). A more scholastic statement of the same doctrine appears in Sermon CCVII in the Ferial Gospel collection. "Þe olde is mater of þis lawe, and þe newe forme þerof. And as mater and forme ben oo þing in substaunce . . . so þe olde lawe and þe newe ben oo þing in substance" (II, 172). Such a view allows very specific interpretation of Old Testament events and practices in view of the New Testament. The passing of the Israelites through the Red Sea, for example, corresponds to the atonement of Christ; the redness of the sea figured the blood of the passion, the stiffness of the wall of water the stability of Christ's godhead, the food in the wilderness, the body and blood of Christ, and the water gushing from the rock which Moses struck the spiritual nourishment offered by Christ (II, 259). Priests of the old law "diden figure of grace þat now is done bi Crist" in that they mediated between God and His people (II, 343). In another light, they are analogues of the disciples, who preached forgiveness, just as the Old Testament priests "telden bi signis of the olde lawe þat men weren cleen of lepre" (I, 18).[25]

The other facet of Wyclif's historical sense has two effects on his presentation of the Biblical narrative. One is the direct substitution of situations and persons in the New Testament for their fourteenth-century counterparts; the other is the tendency to see his own age as degenerate in the face of New Testament glory. The first is expressed in the numerous identifications of Scribes and Pharisees with secular priests and religious, respectively, a device Wyclif employs constantly, both in explicit terms and in casual reference to "our pharisees" or "modern pharisees". The literalness of these applications is often surprising. Christ allowed some of his chosen ones to remain at their "comun lyf" in order "to confounde þes cloistreris; for Crist wiste wel þat þei shulden come and disseyve muche of þis world" (I, 300). Christ's reproof of the Pharisees is glossed thus: "*Þis puple worshipiþ me wiþ þer lippes,* for þei bidden many bedis, *but þeir herte is fer fro me*" (II, 78). The reference to beads suggests the association with religious formality in his own day which the sermon does go on to discuss. Even more explicit is this charge against both religious and secular priests: "Ipocrisie of Pharisees and of Eroude lastiþ ȝit, for newe ordris bigilen þe peple, boþ beggers and possessioneris, in þat þei feynen hem holy to spuyle of hem þe worldli goodis . . . . But ȝit Heroude haþ suteris, as seculers þat now lyven; for as he feynede holynesse in sleying of Joon Baptist, so þei feynen holynesse in pursuying of trewe men" (II, 14). The moral wit of Scripture also has, of course, a positive side: "Of þis dede of Crist men taken, þat it is leveful for to write, and aftirward to rede, a sermoun; for þus dide Crist oure alþer-maistir" (II, 19). The simple fare with which Christ fed the five thousand teaches charity toward the poor rather than indulgence in "strange and likerous mete" (I, 19).

There is also a belief in the decadence of fourteenth-century society and the immanence of the final judgement pervading these sermons. Several explicit formulations of this belief explain the many casual remarks based on it. "It is knowun of bileve", says Wyclif, "þat nyȝ þe ende of þe worlde þe fend temptiþ man faster þan he dide in þe bigynnyng . . .". He urges his people to consider "þe worldis þat weren bifore, how strong and faire men weren þan, and how þe fruytis weren þan good, and now is al turned up so doun" (II, 335). One indication of the general depravity of the age seems to refer to the invention of gunpowder attributed to friar Roger Bacon: "but now men usen a newe craft to slee men comunli, more þan þis craft was usid fro þe tyme þat God was born" (I, 308). Another is the breakdown of what Wyclif envisions as the large, stable empire of New Testament times. "But al þis is passid now; for þe pope and his convent haþ so put doun þe emperour, þat litil rewmes tellen liȝt by him" (I, 316-317). Religious life is also "up so doun" because "in þe laste daies, whan preestis ben turnid to avarice, stonys shal crye and constreyne preestis þat maken hem a privat religioun as an hegge and oþer men þat suen hem in þe brode weye to helleward,—þese stoonys, þat ben myȝty men in þe worlde, shal constreyne boþe preestis and peple for to entre into hevene . . ." (I, 6). So far from Christ's example is the "curiouse preching of Latyn" that "sermouns done lesse good þan þei diden in meke tyme" (II, 19).

Wyclif was indeed the "morning star of the Reformation", but he was also a scholastic debater concerned to support his teachings from Ambrose and Anselm. He was also, as surely, a medieval preacher who knew the importance of the way snakes cover their ears.

1 Margaret Deanesly, *The Lollard Bible* (Cambridge, England, 1920), p. 8.

2 See Gordon Leff, *Heresy in the Later Middle Ages* (Manchester, 1967), II, 494-558.

3 R. L. Poole, *The Dawn of the Reformation* (London, 1905), p. 85.

4 *De Blasphemia, Latin Works,* XII, ed. M. H. Dziewicki (Wyclif Society; London, 1893), 121.

5 *Sermones, Latin Works,* VI, ed. J. Loserth (Wyclif Society; London, 1887), 388.

6 Roundness is attributed to the number five as early as Plutarch's *Moralia* and as late as Thomas Brown's *Garden of Cyrus;* see *Select English Works,* I, 290, n. a.

7 See Sermons 39-43 in *Middle English Sermons,* ed. Woodburn O. Ross (*EETS*, OS, 209) (London, 1940), pp. 220-287.

8 "Wyclif and Hus", *Bulletin John Rylands Library*, L (1966), 387-410.

9 I have counted only the allusions Arnold was able to substantiate; there are hundreds of loosely-worded references to the Bible which are not, strictly speaking, quotations. There are about 130 specific quotations from scripture and 56 from all other sources.

10 Richard McKeon, *Selections from Medieval Philosophers* (New York, 1930), II, xiii.

11 'Pelagian' is Wyclif's term for those theologians who, like Pelagius, placed too much emphasis on man's unaided will. The term may be derived from Bradwardine; see Gordon Leff, *Bradwardine and the Pelagians, Cambridge Studies in Medieval Life and*

Thought, vol. 5 (Cambridge, 1957).

[12] Leff, *Bradwardine,* p. 324.

[13] The 'university' sermons 39-43 in *Middle English Sermons* yield many examples.

[14] MS Douce 321 has "plauntis of soule" (I, 369, n. 1).

[15] *The Life of the Spirit* (New York, 1922), p. 182.

[16] A famous defence of the use of images is found in Reginald Pecock's *Donet,* ed. Elsie Vaughan Hitchcock (*EETS,* OS, 156) (London, 1921), pp. 122-26.

[17] *The Book of Margery Kempe,* ed. Stanford Brown Meech and Hope Emily Allen (*EETS,* OS, 212) (London, 1940), pp. 68, 77-78, 87, 142, 164, 193, 215.

[18] *Literature and the Pulpit in Medieval England* (Cambridge, England, 1933), p. 110-15.

[19] *Festial,* ed. Theodor Erbe (*EETS,* ES, 96) (London, 1905), pp. 98, 121.

[20] II, 500-10.

[21] *Medieval Rhetoric and Poetic* (New York, 1928), p. 239.

[22] *Principles and Problems of Biblical Translation* (Cambridge, England, 1955), p. 46.

[23] Herbert Brook Workman, *John Wyclif: A Study of the English Medieval Church* (Oxford, 1926), I, 101.

[24] *Summa Theologia,* trans. Fathers of the English Dominican Province, I, a, 1 art.x, ad. 3.

[25] See also the interpretation of the burning bush in *Middle English Sermons,* p. 221.

9

CONCLUSION

Although the appreciation of literary artistry is in part a matter of intuition, there are features of a literary surface which can be studied and reported systematically. The minute examination of poems and plays which has borne so much critical fruit recently might with equal success be directed toward the study of prose techniques in Middle English literature. It is particularly important in a case as replete with controversy as Wyclif's to look at the style of the sermons simply to see, after all, what is there.

I have argued that Wyclif does not stand alone at the beginning of the English prose tradition, but rather in company with a large number of competent authors whose several purposes in writing caused them to develop a variety of English styles. The lyricism of the treatises of the mystics, the naivete of the persona of *Mandeville's Travels,* the workmanlike precision of Trevisa's translations, the emotive tenor of Mirk's *exempla*—all have valid claims to excellence in prose style. I have assembled a good deal of evidence to demonstrate, however, that Wyclif brings something distinctive to this tradition. His special bequest to prose is his success in creating homely and idiomatic English expressions for theological and exegetical abstractions. The position he took on the composition of sermons left him no alternative. Rejecting both the overly subtle presentation of the University preachers and the insufficiently Biblical story telling of the friars and their imitators, Wyclif *needed* to create a style for his sermons.

Close study of the texts of his sermons reveals his skill in adopting words and phrases from ordinary speech to translate Scripture. Compared with the two full 'Wycliffite' translations of the Bible, these texts are almost always more idiomatic, concise, unambiguous, and forceful. In the body of the sermons, doctrine is stated and illustrated in simple language. Reproof is couched in bold invective, cutting irony, Biblical allusion, and homely imagery. Although the sermons rarely exhibit a neat thematic unity, they are consistently structured by their use of contrast between the fourteenth-century Church and the teaching of the New Testament. The complex patterns of the sentences are organized, in many cases, by parallelism, balance, and antithesis, a smaller-scale embodiment of the principle of contrast.

Wyclif's allegorical readings of Holy Writ are controlled by their Biblical context and their conformity to the traditional limits of exegesis. They often allow him very effective turns of phrase. The images he himself creates are brief, sharp, and indicative of a close observation of many aspects of life.

Scholasticism inheres in the sermons in their techniques of subdivision, their citation of patristic authority, and their devices of formal logic. The folk imagination is evident in Wyclif's use of feudal guises for Biblical personages, of bestiary materials, of demonology, and of proverbs. Saints' legends are rare and *exempla* altogether absent. The world view which cuts across scholastic and folk elements in medieval thought–the significance of every aspect of the universe because it reveals the plan of God–is also manifested in Wyclif's handling of natural science, etymology and history.

These close and sometimes quantitative approaches to Wyclif's prose revealed aspects of its worth which have seldom, if ever, been noted before. The control and precision I discovered in his irony and invective, belie the traditional charge of rashness. The impersonality of his diction and method cast doubt on the purely biographical explanation of his attempts at reform. The complexity of his syntax runs counter to the usual description of his sentences as simple. The richness and skill of his handling of imagery modifies the charge that he lacked imagination. His thorough acquaintance with and use of the materials of scholasticism and folklore prevent his description as an entirely modern spirit born out of his time. I think there is a real value in these discoveries. They display Wyclif as a more complex and, at the same time, more believable person. They suggest that his contribution to English prose is very great indeed, but many who have praised it in the past have fallen into the error which T. S. Eliot's Becket so wished to avoid; they have done the right thing for the wrong reason.

APPENDIX A

On þe Firste Friday aftir Octave of Twelfþe Day

SERMON CXXXIII

Egressus Jesus.–Luke 4:14

Þis gospel telliþ how Crist prechide, aftir þe storie þat Luk telliþ. *Jesus wente out in vertue of þe Goost in to Galile.* Trewe men trowen as bileve þat þe Holi Gost ledde Jesus whidir ever he wente, and what dedis evere he dide. *And fame wente out þourȝ al þe lond of him; and Crist tauȝte in synagogis of hem, and was magnefied of hem alle. And Crist cam in to Nazareþ, where he was conseyved and nurishid, and he entride bi his custome on Saturdai in to þe synagoge.* And hereof taken Cristene men custome to preche on Sundai, for it comeþ to us for Sabot in þe stede of Saturdai; and Crist hadde custum for to preche on Saturdai, as Luk seiþ here; and so shulden preestis sue him, preching on Sabot þat is Sundai.

And Crist roos up to rede, and þe book of Ysay þe profete was ȝovun to rede. *And as Crist turnede þe book, he fond þe place where it was writun, Þe Spirit of þe Lord is upon me, wherfore he anoyntide me; to preche to po*[illegible] *men he sente me,* and so þe Holi Goost bad me, *preche to prisoneris forȝyvenes, and to blynde men siȝt, to leeve broken men in remissioun, to preche þe ȝeer þat þe Lord acceptiþ, and þe dai of aȝenȝyvyng.* Þis preching is al disusid, and turnid to pride and coveitise. For how ever men mai plese þe peple, and wiþ moneie wynne hem worship, þat þei prechen, and putten abak þe profit of þe peplis soule. Þis book was ordeyned of God to be red in þis place, for alle þingis þat felden to Crist weren ordeyned for to come þus. And so men seyen Crist hadde office of alle þe mynystris in þe Chirche. Crist lernede to rede whanne he wolde, and he preiside mouche Ysay; and þes eiȝte wordis red here of Crist han betere ordre þan we can telle; for þe Hooli Goost was on Crist boþe in his bodi and soule, siþ Crist was boþe God and man, and bi his manheed led of God. And þerfore þis Goost anoyntide Crist wiþ goodis of grace as fulli as ony man myȝte be anoyntid. And þus Crist mut nedis preche to meke men þat wolden take it, for þis is þe beste dede þat man doiþ here to his breþeren. And so Crist prechide, to prisoneris forȝyvyng of þer synnes, and to men blinde in wit, for to knowe þe wille of God, and leeve broken men in forȝyvenesse of þer travaile. And Crist prechide þe ȝeer of our Lord þat was acceptable bi him; for he made the ȝeer Jubile; and daie of ȝyvyng of mercy and of blis was prechid of Crist. And so alle þes eiȝte wordis sownen in mercy and confort of Crist, to men þat ben in prisoun here for olde synnes þat þei have done.

And whanne Crist hadde folden þis book, he ȝaf it to þe servaunt, and he sat; and þe eyen of alle þat weren in þe sinagoge weren loking to him. And Crist bigan to seie to hem, Þat þis dai is þis writing fild in ȝour iȝen on me. For Isay seide þes wordis, as men þat profecieden of Crist. *And alle men ȝaven him witnesse; and alle men woundriden in þe wordis of grace þat camen of his mouþ.* Of þis dede of Crist men taken, þat it is leveful for to write, and aftirward to rede, a sermoun; for þus dide Crist oure alþer-maistir. For ȝif men mai þus turne þe peple, what shulde lette to have þis maner? Certis traveile of þe prechour or name of havyng of good witt shulde not be þe ende of preching, but profit to þe soule of þe peple; and however þis ende comeþ beste, is moost plesing to God. And curiouse preching of Latyn is ful fer fro þis ende; for many men prechen hemsilf, and leeve to preche Jesus Crist; and so sermouns done lesse good þan þei diden in meke tyme, (II, 17-19).

APPENDIX B: TABLE OF SENTENCE LENGTHS

Number of Sentences Containing the Indicated Number of Words

	1-10	11-20	21-30	31-40	41-50	51-60	61-70	71-80	81-90	91-100	101-110	111-120
I		13	13	11	11	8	5	2	3	5	2	1
II	1	15	26	24	22	14	4	1	3			
III	14	66	83	39	16	9	2	1	1	1		
IV	1	20	33	15	5	4		1				
V	8	32	66	28	10	11	1	1		1		

I *Evangelia Dominicalia*, Sermons I-III
II *Commune Sanctorum*, Sermons LV-LVIII
III *Proprium Sanctorum*, Sermons LXXXVI-LXXXVIII
IV Ferial Gospels, Sermons CXXIV-CXXVI
V Sunday Epistles, Sermons I-III

Line 1 shows the wide spread of lengths of sentences in the sermons of the first group printed by Arnold. Note that there is no clustering around the average figure, which for this group is 42.87. The sentences of the other four groups (lines 2-5) contain an average of 28.78 words and are distributed more nearly like a normal curve.

APPENDIX C

Evangelia Dominicalis Sermon I (I, 1-3).

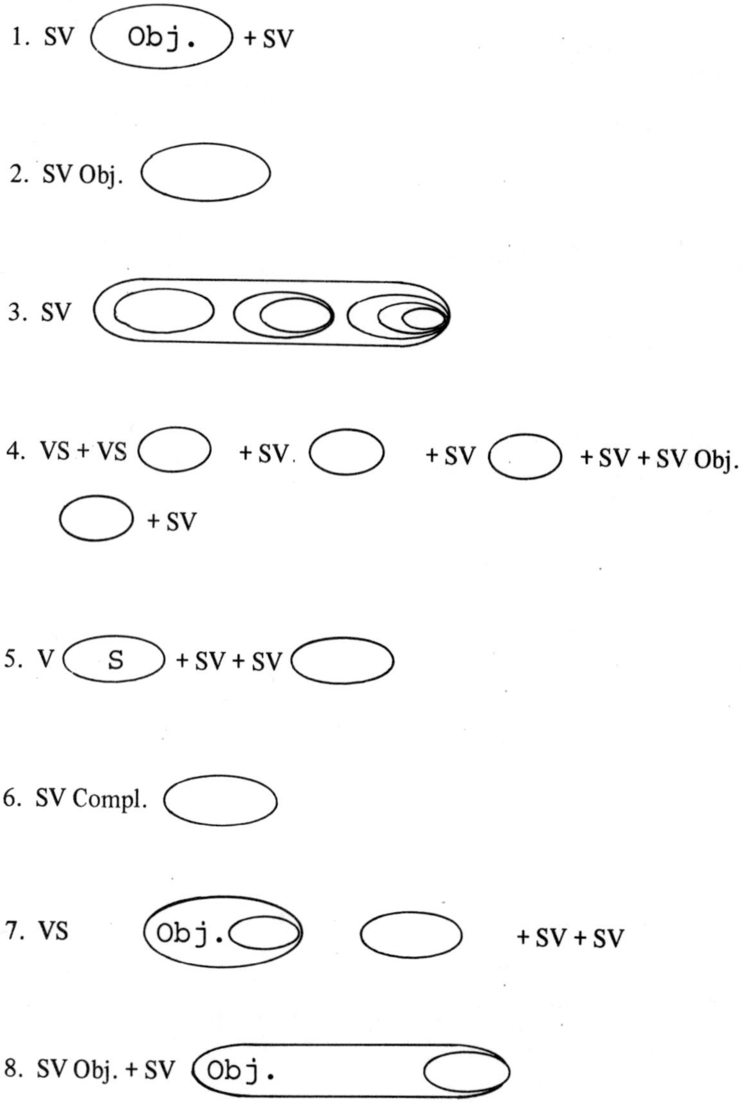

1. SV (Obj.) + SV

2. SV Obj.

3. SV

4. VS + VS + SV + SV + SV + SV Obj. + SV

5. V (S) + SV + SV

6. SV Compl.

7. VS (Obj.) + SV + SV

8. SV Obj. + SV (Obj.)

9. 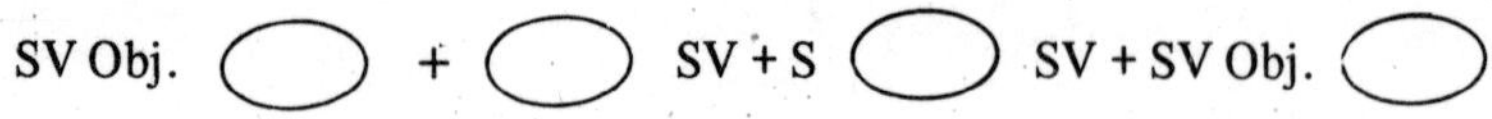 SV Obj. ⬭ + ⬭ SV + S ⬭ SV + SV Obj. ⬭

10. 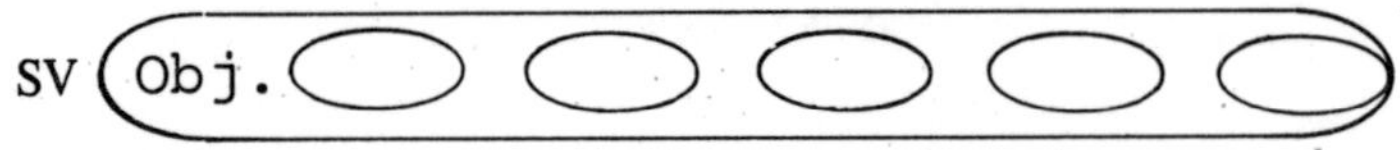 SV (Obj. ⬭ ⬭ ⬭ ⬭ ⬭)

11. 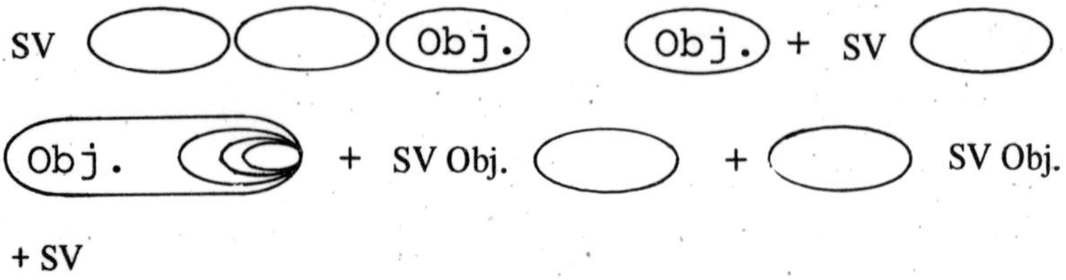 SV ⬭ ⬭ (Obj.) (Obj.) + SV ⬭

(Obj. ⬭) + SV Obj. ⬭ + ⬭ SV Obj.

+ SV

12. 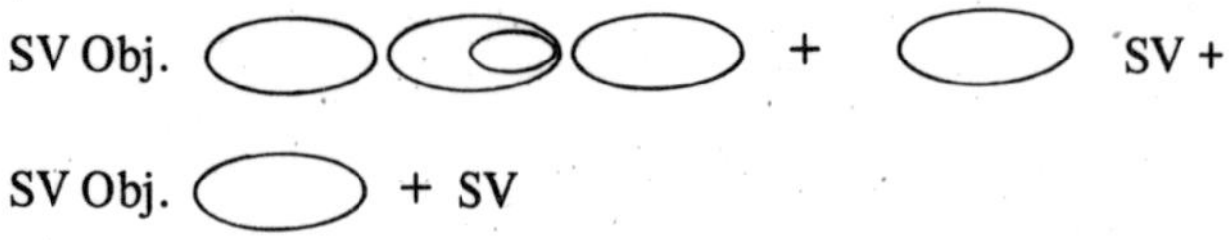 SV Obj. ⬭ ⬭ ⬭ + ⬭ SV +

SV Obj. ⬭ + SV

13. 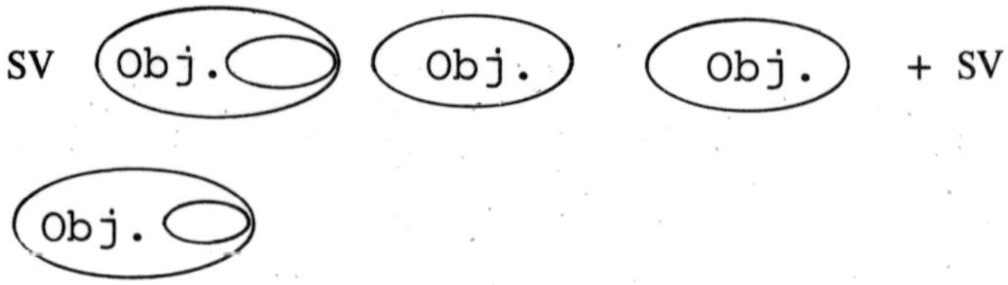 SV (Obj. ⬭) (Obj.) (Obj.) + SV

(Obj. ⬭)

14. 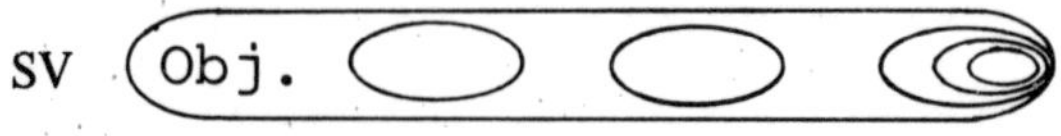 SV (Obj. ⬭ ⬭ ⬭)

15.  VS ⬭

16.  VS (Obj. ⬭ ⬭) + SV (Obj.)

Gospel Sermon I (I, 1-4).

1. 

2. SV Obj.

3. SV Obj. 

4. SV Obj. + VS Obj. ?

5. Obj. VS 

6. VS Compl.

7. SV

8. SV Compl. + SV

9. VS Obj.

10. 

11. VS + SV

12. SV

13. SV

14. SV Obj. Obj.

15. SV Obj.

16. SV Compl. + SV Compl.

Gospel Sermon I (I, 1-4).

17. SV Obj.

18. SV Compl.

19. SV Compl.

20. SV Compl.

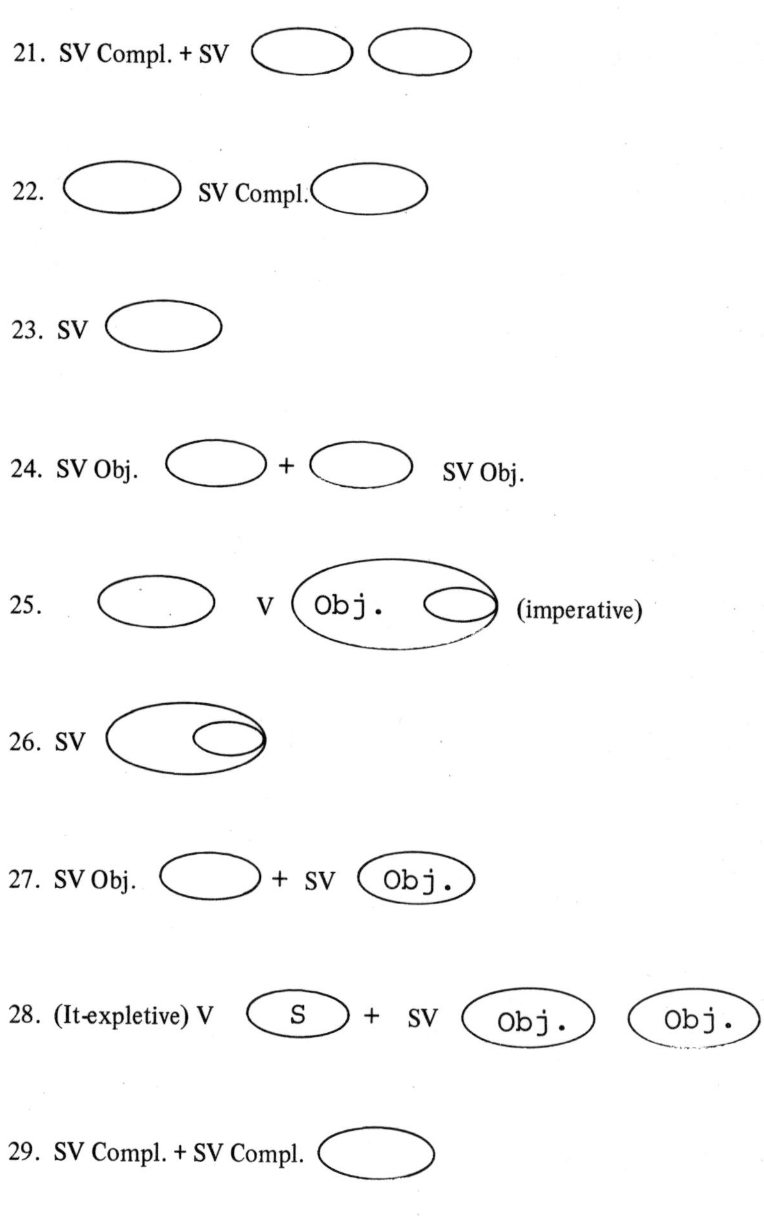
21. SV Compl. + SV
22. SV Compl.
23. SV
24. SV Obj. + SV Obj.
25. V Obj. (imperative)
26. SV
27. SV Obj. + SV Obj.
28. (It-expletive) V S + SV Obj. Obj.
29. SV Compl. + SV Compl.
30. SV
31. SV Compl.

32. SV + SV + SV ⬭

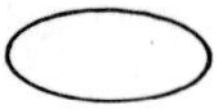

Gospel Sermon I (I, 1-4)

33. SV

34. (It-expletive) V (S ⬭) +SV Obj.

35. SV

36. SV Obj.  ⬭ + Obj. VS

37. VS ⬭ ⬭ +VS Obj.  ⬭ ?

38.  ⬭ SV ⬭ + SV

39. SV (⬭)

40. SV Obj. + XV Obj.

41. SV ⬭ + SV Compl. + SV Compl. + SV Compl. + Obj. VS ⬭

Epistolae Dominicales Sermon I (II, 221-225)

1. SV 

2. SV Obj.

3. SV

4. SV Obj.

5. SV Obj.

6. SV

7. Obj. VS + SV

8. SV Obj.

9. SV Obj. + SV

10. SV Obj.

11. Obj. VS

12. SV Obj.

13. SV

14. SV Obj.

15. VS

16. SV Compl. + SV

17. S V

18. (It-expletive) V S

19. (It-expletive) V S

20. SV Obj. + VS

21. VS (analyzed on p. 118)

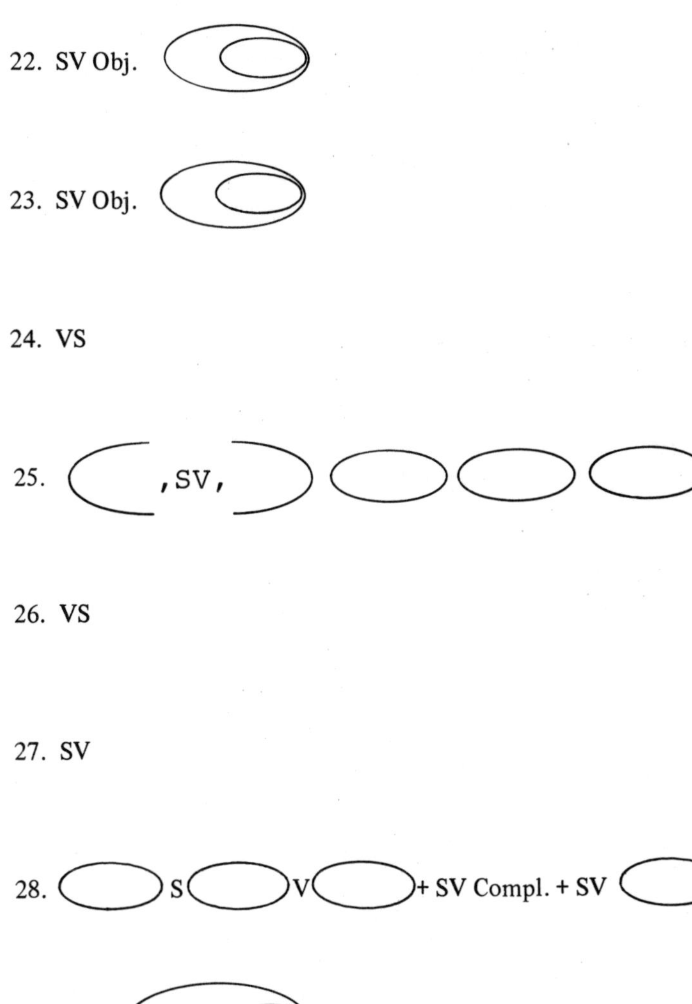

30. VS + VS +VS +SV

31. SV

32. SV Obj.

33. 

34. S V Compl.

35. SV Obj. 

36. 

37. SV 

38. VS

39. (It-expletive) V 

40. SV Obj.

41. SV Obj.

42. SV Obj.

43. VS

44. SV Obj. + SV Compl. + SV Compl.

45. VS

46. SV Obj.

47. S V

48. VS Obj.

49. SV + SV Obj.

50. SV + Obj. VS

51. S V Compl.

52. SV Obj. + SV Obj. + VS

53. SV Compl.

54. SV

55. VS Compl. + SV

56. SV Obj.

58. SV Compl.

59. SV Compl.

60. SV

61. SV

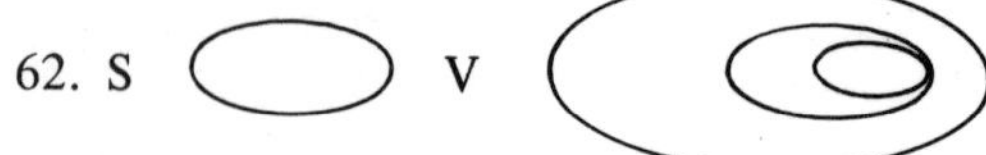

63. (It-expletive) V S

64. SV

BIBLIOGRAPHY

Aquinas, Thomas, *Summa Theologica,* trans., Fathers of the English Dominican Province.

Bagster, Samuel, *The English Hexapla* (London, 1841).

Bainton, Roland H., *Early and Medieval Christianity* (Boston, 1962).

Baldwin, Charles Sears, *Medieval Rhetoric and Poetic* (New York, 1928).

Bennett, H. S., "Fifteenth Century Secular Prose", *RES*, XXI (1945), 257-263.

Bethurum, Dorothy, ed. *Critical Approaches to Medieval Literature.* (New York, 1960).

Block, Edward A., *John Wyclif, Radical Dissenter* (San Diego State College Press, 1962) (*Humanities Monograph Series,* Vol. I, no. I).

Brady, Sister Mary Teresa, R.D.C. "The Apostles' Creed in the Manuscripts of *The Pore Caitif", Speculum,* XXXII (1957), 323-325.

Brown, Beatrice Daw, "Religious Lyrics in MS. Don. c. 13", *Bodleian Quarterly Record,* VII (March 1932).

Bühler, C. F., "A Lollard Tract on Translating the Bible in English", *Med. Aev.* (Oct. 1938), 167-183.

_____, "The Middle English Texts of Morgan MS 861", *PLMA* LXIX (1954), 686-692.

Burrows, Montagu, *Wyclif's Place in History* (Oxford, 1881).

Cadman, Samuel Parkes, *The Three Religious Leaders of Oxford and Their Movements* (New York, 1916).

Cambridge Bibliography of English Literature, ed. F. W. Bateson, 4 vols. (Cambridge, 1941).

The Cambridge Medieval History, ed. H. M. Gwatkin, et al., vol. 2 (Cambridge, 1911-36).

Caplan, Harry C., "Classical Rhetoric and the Medieval Theory of Preaching", *Classical Philology* (April 1933), 73-96.

_____, "The Four Senses of Scriptural Interpretation and the Medieval Theory of Preaching", *Speculum,* IV (1929), 282-290.

_____, "Rhetorical Invention in Some Medieval Tractites on Preaching", *Speculum,* II (1927), 284-295.

Carrick, John Charles, *Wycliffe and the Lollards.* (Edinburgh, 1908).

Chambers, R. W., *Man's Unconquerable Mind.* (London, 1939).

_____, *On the Continuity of English Prose.* (*EETS*, OS, 186) (London, 1932).

Chapman, C. O., "Chaucer on Preachers and Preaching", *PLMA,* XLIV (1929), 178-185.

_____, "The Parson's Tale: A Medieval Sermon", *MLN,* XLIII (1928), 229-234.

Chaucer, Geoffrey, *The Complete Works of Chaucer,* ed. Fred N. Robinson, 2nd ed. (Cambridge, Mass., 1957).

Chronicon Henrici Knighton, ed. Joseph Rawson Lumby, 2 vols. (London, 1889).

Cloud of Unknowing and the Book of Privy Counselling, ed. Phyllis Hodgson (*EETS,* OS, 218) (London, 1874-93).

Colledge, Eric, *The Medieval Mystics of England* (New York, 1961).

_____, *"The Recluse:* A Lollard Interpolated Version of the *Ancrene Riwle*", *RES* XV (1939), 1-15, 129-145.

Coulton, G. G., *Medieval Panorama* (Cambridge, 1938).

Cumming, W. P., "A Middle English M.S. in the Bibliothèque Ste. Genevieve, Paris", *PLM*, XLII (1927), 862-864.

Cutts, Cecilia, "The Croxton Play: An Anti-Lollard Piece", *MLQ*, (March 1944), 45-60.
Dahmus, Joseph Henry, "John Wyclif and the English Government", *Speculum* XXXV (1960), 51-68.
——, *The Prosecution of Wyclif* (New Haven, 1952).
——, "Wyclif was a Negligent Pluralist", *Speculum*, XXVIII (1953), 378-381.
Daly, L. J., S. J., *The Political Theory of John Wyclif* (Chicago, 1962).
Deane, D. J., *Two Noble Lives: John Wicliffe and Martin Luther* (London, n.d.).
Deanesly, Margaret, *A History of the Medieval Church 590-1500* (London, 1951).
——, *The Lollard Bible* (Cambridge, England, 1920).
——, *The Significance of the Lollard Bible* (London, 1951).
——, "Vernacular Books in England in the Fourteenth and Fifteenth Centuries", *MLR*, XV (1920), 349-358.
Dictionary of National Biography, ed. Leslie Stephen and Sidney Lee, 63 vols. (London, 1885-1900).
du Pont Breck, Allen, *Johannis Wyclyf Tractatus de Trinitate* (Boulder, Colorado, 1962).
"England in the Time of Wyclif", ed. Edward P. Cheyney, *Translations and Reprints from the Original Sources of European History*, vol. II, no. 5, (Philadelphia, 1895).
English Association, *The Year's Work in English Studies* (1919-) (London, 1921).
Forshall, Josiah and Madden, Sir Frederic, *The Holy Bible* (*Oxford Bible*, vol. 4) (London, 1850).
Foxe, John, *Acts and Monuments* (London, 1583).
——, *Book of Martyrs*, 3 vols. (London, 1641).
Fristedt, Sven L., *The Wycliffe Bible* (Stockholm, 1953).
Fowler, David C. "John Trevisa and the English Bible", *MP*, LVIII (Nov. 1960), 81-98.
Gairdner, James, *Lollardy and the Reformation in England*, 4 vols. (London, 1908-1913).
Gasquet, Francis Aiden, *The Old English Bible and Other Essays* (London, 1897).
Gilmour, J., "A Note on the Vocabulary of Richard Rolle", *NQ* (1956).
Gilpin, William, *The Lives of John Wicliffe and of the Most Eminent of His Disciples* (London, 1766).
Gilson, Etienne, "Michel Menot et la technique du sermon médiéval", *Revue d'histoire franciscaine* II, no. 3 (July 1925), 301ff.
——, *Reason and Revelation in the Middle Ages*. New York, 1939.
Gospels, Gothic, Anglo-Saxon, Wycliffe, and Tyndale Versions, ed. Joseph Bosworth and George Waring, 4th ed. (London, 1907).
Goss, J. Harold, *Semasiological Notes on the Wycliffite Hebrews*, M.A. Thesis (U. of Pittsburgh, 1932).
Green, S. G., *Wycliffe Anecdotes, or Incidents and Characteristics from the Life of the Great English Reformer*, Religious Tract Society (London, n.d.).
Three Middle English Sermons from the Worcester Manuscript FL0, ed. D. M. Grisdale (*Leeds School of Engl. Lang. Texts and Monographs*, No. 5).
Gwynn, Aubrey Osborne, *The English Austin Friars in the Time of Wyclif* (Oxford, 1940).
Hale, Edward E., Jr., "Ideas on Rhetoric in the Sixteenth Century", *PLMA* XVIII (1908), 424-444.
Hargreaves, Henry, "From Bede to Wyclif: Medieval English Bible Translations", *BJRL*, XLVIII (1965-66), 118-140.
——, "Wyclif's Prose", *E & S*, XIX (1966), 1-17.
Heffernan, Sister Mary Antonia, C.I.M., *A Man and His Errors*, M.A. Thesis (Duquesne University, Pittsburgh, 1925.
Herrick, S. E., *Some Heretics of Yesterday* (London, 1885).
Hexter, J. H., "The Loom of Language and the Fabric of Imperatives: The Case of *Il Principe* and *Utopia*", *American Historical Review* LXIX, no. 4 (July 1964), 945-968.
Hilton, Walter, *The Sermon which Christ Made on the Way to Emaus* (London, 1879).

Hodgson, Phyllis, "A Ladder of Foure Ronges", *MLR,* XLIV (Oct. 1949), 465-475.

Holt, Emily Sarah, *John de Wycliffe and What He Did for England* (London, n.d.).

Irvine, Annie S., "The Participle in Wyclif", *Univ. of Texas Bulletin* (July 8, 1929).

——, "The To Comyng(e) Construction in Wyclif", *PLMA*, XLV (June 1930), 468-500.

Jacob's Well, ed. Arthur Brandeis (*EETS*, OS, 115) (London, 1900).

James, Thomas, *An Apology for John Wyclif* (Oxford, 1608).

Jones, Edmund, D., "Authenticity of Some English Works Ascribed to Wyclif", *Anglia* 30 (1907), 261-268.

Jusserand, Jean J., *A Literary History of the English People* (New York, London, 1895), vol. I, 422-438.

Kennedy, A. G., *A Bibliography of Studies on the English Language* (Cambridge, Mass., 1959).

Kemp, M. B., *The Book of Margery Kemp,* ed. Stanford B. Meech and Hope Emily Allen (*EETS*, OS, 212) (London, 1940).

Ker, W. P., *Medieval English Literature* (London, 1912).

Knowles, David, *The English Mystical Tradition* (New York, 1961).

——, *The Religious Orders of England* (Cambridge, England, 1955).

——, *Saints and Scholars: Twenty-five Medieval Portraits* (Cambridge, England, 1962).

Krapp, G. P., *The Rise of English Literary Prose* (Oxford, New York, 1915).

Lay Folks Mass Book, ed. Thomas Frederick Simmons (*EETS,* OS, 71) (London, 1879).

Le Bas, Charles Webb, *The Life of John Wiclif* (London, 1832).

Lechler, G. V., *John Wycliffe and His English Precursors,* trans. J. Lorimer (London, 1884).

Leff, Gordon, *Bradwardine and the Pelagians* (*Cambridge Studies in Medieval Life and Thought,* vol. 5) (Cambridge, England, 1957).

——, *Heresy in the Later Middle Ages* (Manchester, 1967).

——, "Wyclif and Hus: A Doctrinal Comparison", *BJRL*,L (1958), 387-410.

Lewis, C. S., *The Allegory of Love* (London, 1938).

Lewis, John, *The History of the Life and Sufferings of John Wycliff* (London, 1720).

——, *The New Testament Translation of John Wycliff* (London, 1731).

Loserth, Johann, *Wyclif and Hus* (London, 1884).

Lovejoy, Arthur O., *The Great Chain of Being* (New York, 1936).

McFarlane, Kenneth Bruce, *John Wycliffe and the Beginnings of English Nonconformity* (London, 1952).

Mallard, William, "Dating the *Sermones Quadraginta* of John Wyclif", *M & H,* XVII (1968), 86-104.

——, "John Wyclif and the Tractate 'Of Biblical Authority' ", *Church History* XXX (March 1961), 50-60.

Mandeville's Travels, ed. P. Hamelius (*EETS*, OS, 153) (London, 1919).

Manning, Bernard Lord, *The People's Faith in the Time of Wyclif* (Cambridge, England, 1919).

Marsh, G. P., *Lectures in The English Language,* 4th ed. (New York, 1874).

Matthew, Fredric D., *Life of John Wycliffe* (London, n.d.).

McKeon, Richard, ed., *Selections from Medieval Philosophers,* 2 vols. (New York, 1929).

Middle English Dictionary, Hans Kurath and Sherman M. Kuhn, ed. of Part C6 (Ann Arbor, Michigan, 1952).

Middle English Sermons, ed. Woodburn O. Ross (*EETS*, OS, 209) (London, 1940).

Mirk, John. *Instructions for Parish Priests,* ed. E. Peacock, (*EETS,* 31) (London).

——, *Festial,* ed. Theodor Erbe (*EETS,* ES, 96) (London, 1905).

Moeller, Wilhelm, *History of the Christian Church in the Middle Ages,* trans. Andrew Rutherford (London, 1893).

Morgan, Margery, "*A Talking of the Love of God* and the Continuity of M. E. Prose Meditations", *RES,* XXVIII (April 1952), 97-116.

——, "A Treatise in Cadence", *MLR* (April 1952), 156-164.

Morrall, John B., *Political Thought in Medieval Times* (New York, 1960).

Mosher, Joseph Albert, *The Exemplum in the Early Religious and Didactic Literature of England* (New York, 1911).

Mustanoja,, Tauno F., *A Middle English Syntax* (Helsinki, 1960).

Netter, Thomas, *Fasciculi Zizaniorum*, ed. Walter Waddington Shirley (London, 1858).

A New English Dictionary on Historical Principles, ed. James A. H. Murray, et al., 10 vols. (Oxford, 1888-1928).

The New Testament in English, ed. Walter W. Skeat from the Forshall and Madden edition of the Bible (London, 1879).

Ohlander, Urban, *Studies on Co-ordinate Expressions in Middle English* (*Lund Studies in English*, V) (London, 1936).

Owst, G. R., *Literature and the Pulpit in Medieval England* (Cambridge, England, 1933).

———, *Preaching in Medieval England* (Cambridge, England, 1926).

Pantin, W. A., *The English Church in the Fourteenth Century* (Cambridge, England, 1955).

Peacock, Reginald, *Donet*, ed. Elsie Vaughan Hitchcock (*EETS*, OS, 156) (London, 1921).

———, *The Reule of Crysten Religioun* (*EETS*, OS, 171) (London, 1927).

Pennington, Arthur R., *John Wyclif: His Life, Times, and Teaching* (London, 1884).

Pfander, H. G., "The Medieval Friars and Some Alphabetical Reference Books for Sermons", *Medium Aevum*, III (Feb. 1934), 19-30.

———, *The Popular Sermon of the Medieval Friar in England*, New York University Dissertation.

Phillimore, J. S., "Blessed Thomas More and the Arrest of Humanism in England", *Dublin Review*, CLIII (1913), 1-17.

Poole, Reginald Lane, *Wycliffe and Movements for Reform* (London, 1889).

———, *Illustrations of the History of Medieval Thought and Learning*, 2nd ed. (London, 1920).

Power, Eileen, *Medieval People*, 9th ed. (London, 1950).

Rashdall, Hastings, *Medieval Universities*, ed. Powicke and Emden (Oxford, 1936).

Reeves, W. Peters, "A Second MS of Wyclif's 'De Dominio Civili' ", *MLN*, L (Feb. 1935), 96-98.

Rickert, Edith, *Chaucer's World* (New York, 1962).

Robson, John Adam, *Wyclif and the Oxford Schools* (Cambridge, England, 1961).

Rolle, Richard, *English Writings of Richard Rolle*, ed. Hope Emily Allen (Oxford, 1931).

———, *English Prose Treatises of Richard Rolle of Hampole*, ed. George C. Perry (*EETS*, OS, 20) (London, 1886).

Savage, Henry L., Review of *Wyclif, Select English Writings* (Winn), *MLN*, XLVI (1931), 64-66.

Schmidt, Fredrik, *The Language of Peacock* (Upsala. 1900).

Schwarz, W., *Principles and Problems of Biblical Translation* (Cambridge, England, 1955).

Sergeant, Lewis, *John Wyclif, Last of the Schoolmen and First of the English Reformers* (New York, 1892).

Shettle, G. T., *John Wyclif of Wycliffe and Other Essays* (Leeds, 1922).

Shirley, Walter Waddington, *Catalogue of the Original Works of John Wyclif* (Oxford, 1865).

Simon, H., "Chaucer A Wyclifite", *Chaucer Soc. Essays*, Ser. II, No. 17, 227-292.

Smalley, Beryl, *The Study of the Bible in the Middle Ages* (London, 1941).

Smith, Lucy Toulmin, "English Popular Preaching in the Fourteenth Century", *English Historical Review*, VII (1892), 25-36.

Speculum Christiani, ed. G. Holmstedt (*EETS*, OS, 182) (London, 1929).

Spinks, Matthew, *Advocates of Reform: from Wyclif to Erasmus* (*Library of Christian Classics*, XIV) (1953).

Stein, I. H., "Another 'Lost' Chapter of Wyclif's *Summa de Ente*", *Speculum*, VIII (Oct. 1933), 254-255.

———, "The Latin Text of Wyclif's 'Complaint' ", *Speculum*, VII (Jan. 1932), 87-94.

———, "An Unpublished Fragment of Wyclif's 'Confessio'", *Speculum*, VII (Oct. 1933), 503-510.

———, "Two Notes on Wyclif", *Speculum*, VI (July 1931), 465-468.

———, "The Wyclif Manuscript in Florence", *Speculum*, V (Jan. 1930), 95-97.

Stevenson, Joseph, S. J., *The Truth about John Wyclif* (London, 1885).

Storrs, Richard Salter, *John Wycliffe and the English Bible* (New York, 1880).

Talbert, E. W., "The Date of the Composition of the English Wycliffite Collection of Sermons", *Speculum*, XII (Oct. 1937), 464-474.

———, "A Lollard Chronicle of the Papacy", *JEGP*, XLI (April 1942), 163-193.

Tatlock, J. S. P., "Chaucer and Wyclif", *MP*, XIV (1916), 257-268.

Taylor, Henry Osborne, *The Medieval Mind* (Cambridge, Mass., 1925).

Thomson, S. Harrison, "A Gonville and Caius Wyclif Manuscript", *Speculum*, VII (April 1933), 197-204.

———, "Some Latin Works Erroneously Ascribed to Wyclif", *Speculum*, III (1928), 382-391.

———, "Summa de Ente", *Speculum*, IV (July 1929), 339-346.

———, "Three Unprinted Opuscula of John Wyclif", *Speculum*, III (April 1928), 248-253.

———, "Unnoticed Manuscripts of Wyclif's *De Veritate Sacre Scripture", Medium Aevum*, XII (1943), 68-70.

———, " 'Wyclif' or 'Wyclyf' ", *English Historical Review*, LIII (1938), 675-678.

Thoresby, John, *Lay Folks Catechism*, ed. T. F. Simmons and H. E. Nolloth (*EETS*, 188).

Trevelyan, George Macaulay, *England in the Age of Wycliffe* (London, 1904).

Trevisa, John, *Dialogues inter Militem et Clericum.* ed. A. J. Perry (*EETS*, OS, 167) (London, 1925).

Twemlow, J. A., "Wyclif's Preferments and University Degrees", *English Historical Review*, XV (1900), 529-530.

Underhill, Evelyn, *The Life of the Spirit* (New York, 1922).

Vaughan, Ralph, *The Life and Opinions of John de Wycliffe* (London, 1831).

Vulgate New Testament with the Douay Version of 1582 in Parallel Columns (London, 1872).

Weinberg, Julius, *A Short History of Medieval Philosophy* (Princeton, 1964).

Wells, John E., *A Manual of the Writings in Middle English, 1050-1400* (New Haven, 1916), Supplements, 9 vols. (New Haven, 1919-52).

White, Helen C., *Social Criticism in Popular Religious Literature of the Sixteenth Century* (New York, 1944).

Wilson, R. M. "Three Medieval Mystics", *E & S*, NS, IX (1956), 95.

Winn, Herbert E., *Wyclif, Select English Writings* (London, 1929).

Workman, Herbert Brook, *The Dawn of the Reformation* (London, 1933).

———, *John Wyclif: a Study of the Medieval Church* (Oxford, 1926).

Wilkins, Henry John, *Was John Wycliffe a Negligent Pluralist?* (London, New York, 1915).

Wyclif, John, *An Apology for Lollard Doctrines* (Camden Soc. Publ., London, 1842).

———, *The English Works of John Wyclif, Hitherto Unprinted*, ed. F. D. Matthew (*EETS*, OS, 74) (London, 1880).

———, *The Lanterne of Liȝt*, ed. Lillian M. Swinburn (*EETS*, OS, 151) (London, 1917).

———, *Latin Works* (Wyclif Society, London):

de Apostasia, IX. ed., M. H. Dziewicki, 1889.

de Benedicta Incarnacione, VI. ed. H. Harris, 1886.

de Blasphemia, XIII. ed. M. H. Dziewicki, 1893.

de Civili Domino, II. ed. R. L. Poole and J. Loserth, 1885-1900.

de Compositione Hominis, III. ed. R. Beer, 1884.

de Dominio Divinio, X. ed. R. L. Poole, 1890.

de Ecclesia, IV. ed. J. Loserth, 1886.
de Ente Praedicamentali, XI. ed. R. Beer, 1891.
de Eucharistia, XII. ed. J. Loserth, 1892.
de Officio Regis, VIII. ed. A. W. Pollard and C. Sayle, 1887.
de Potestate Pape, III. ed. J. Loserth, 1907.
Dialogus sine Speculum Ecclesiae Militantis, V. ed. R. Buddenseig, 1907-09.
Polemical Works in Latin, I. ed. R. Buddenseig, 1883.
Sermones, VI. ed. J. Loserth, 1887.

——, *Select English Works,* ed. Thomas Arnold (Oxford, 1869-71).

——, *Summa de Ente.* ed. S. Harrison Thomson (London, 1930).

——, *Wicklieffes Wicket* (London, 1548).

Wyld, H. C., "Some Aspects of Style and Idiom in Fifteenth Century English", *Essays and Studies,* XXVI (1940), 30-44.

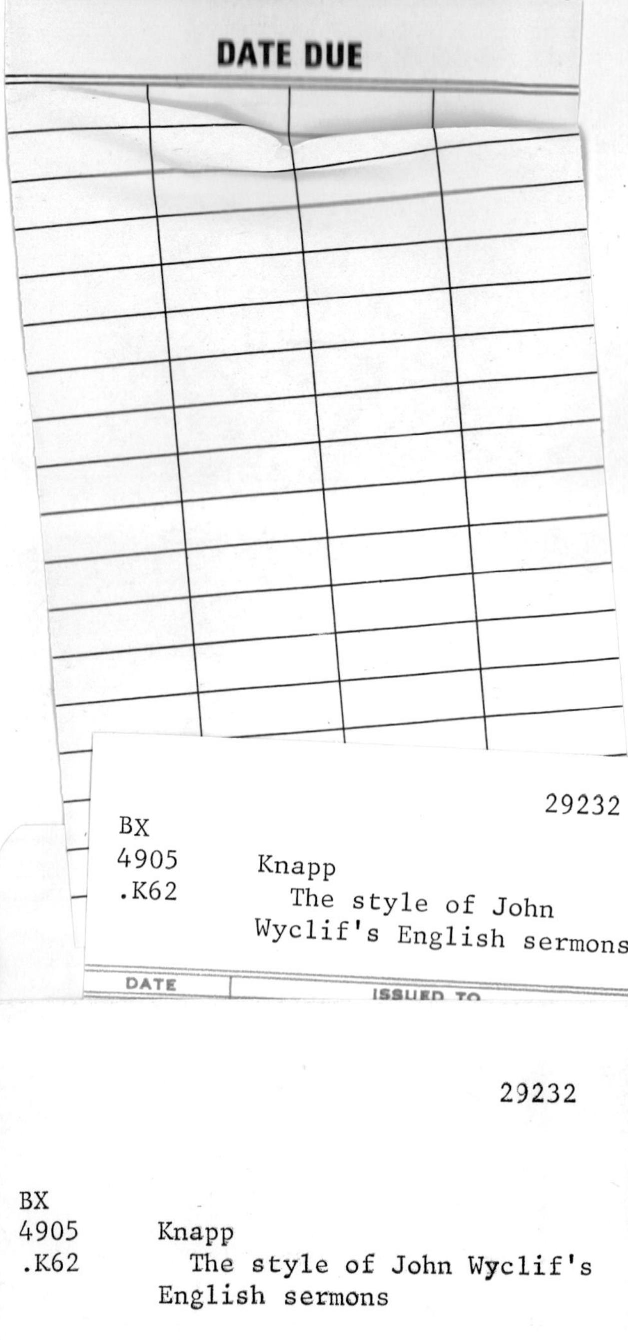

29232
BX
4905
.K62
Knapp
The style of John Wyclif's
English sermons